Walking with Grace

Tools for Implementing and Launching a Congregational Respite Program

Robin Dill

iUniverse, Inc.
New York Bloomington

iUniverse books may be ordered through booksellers or by contacting:

iUniverse
1663 Liberty Drive
Bloomington, IN 47403
www.iuniverse.com
1-800-Authors (1-800-288-4677)

ISBN: 978-1-4401-3063-2 (sc)
ISBN: 978-1-4401-3062-5 (ebook)

Printed in the United States of America

iUniverse rev. date: 03/10/09

Dedication

It is to all those people at Grace Arbor that I dedicate this manual. To the volunteers and my assistant director, Cindy Leake, who work tirelessly to love and support our participants, I give you thanks! You all have taught me so much. To the caregivers of these precious participants who are putting their lives on hold and caring 24/7, I am humbly grateful to walk with you on this journey. To the incredible participants of Grace Arbor who bring me joy, laughter, love, acceptance, and learning, I give you my profound appreciation!

Acknowledgements

Much prayer, time, thought, and encouragement have gone into writing this manual. It is amazing to think how God uses experiences in our daily lives to create an opportunity for ministry. Cancer has been a huge teacher in my life as I have walked beside my mother and husband as they experienced this horrible disease firsthand. Lessons in caregiving broadened my Stephen Ministry training as it now became personal. From these experiences, as well as doing pastoral care at two Atlanta area hospitals (plus a thousand other things!), I came to apply for the job to implement, launch, and direct an Older Adult Day program at First United Methodist Church in Lawrenceville Georgia.

My dream is that "The Church" will see clearly its role in health care for the family. The church has the unique opportunity to provide care to older adults in a loving, compassionate way. By utilizing members' spiritual gifts, talents, resources, and energy, a vibrant and successful program can be birthed and run. I have witnessed this firsthand and now have a way to share those experiences and knowledge gained.

I want to take the time to thank the many people who have helped this project become a reality and, hopefully, a viable resource for others:

My sister, **Jane**, who first shared her vision about my writing a book and encouraged me to write

My husband, **Tom**, who was the first to read through my manuscript and helped me see that it was worth trying to get published. His faithful prayers have kept me going in the months of writing and editing!

My sister, **Linda,** the editing guru who has offered many suggestions and encouragement and who after reading this manual decided to take time out of her life to see Grace Arbor in action

My administrative assistant, **Nancy Ford,** another editing guru whose attention to detail has been a huge asset, not only in this manual, but in our ministry together at Grace Arbor

Sheri Smith, minister of Congregational Care who was one who has believed in me and my ministry from the start

Helon Gragg, whose sound advice and expertise have given me guidance and direction in the editing and publishing process

Cindy Leake, assistant director of Grace Arbor, and all the volunteers who have undergirded me in prayer through the writing, editing and publishing process

My dad, **Bill Wunch**, who cared lovingly for my mom Lois as she slipped away into dementia brought about by brain cancer. He gave me encouragement in the writing process.

Lastly, my two adult children, **David** and **Leslie**, who have spent hours listening and serving at Grace Arbor, as well as praying for their mom!

Soli Deo Gloria!
Robin Dill
November 2008

Cover Design
David Dill

Editorial Consultant
Helon Gragg

Those of you who are reading this with the weight of Ministry on your shoulders are aware of the blessing that this book will be to those who need it most. If Robin had been able to order this book and read it before she began Grace Arbor, she may have either run as fast as she could in the other direction, or she would have had a much-needed and useful tool to help her do the work that she is doing. I pray that this book will be that tool for each of you as you seek to serve those in your midst with memory impairment. I firmly believe that God speaks clearly through those who can least remember what happened just 10 minutes ago, because he doesn't have to wade through all the excuses for why they cannot be completely candid about how they feel or what they think, as the rest of us do. The participants of Grace Arbor are the role models for my life; as they chase their illusive memories, they grow and become aware of how God helps them through each day. I want to be in love with Jesus and serve him as willingly and openly as they do all the days of my life.

Robin astounds me daily with her ability to take time out of her busy life and ministry to write this book as well as leading a healthy and growing program. I am so blessed to know her and to be able to sit at her feet in awe as I read this book and see her heart revealed in its pages. Please take all the time you need to absorb the planning and love that has gone into providing the program that led to this working guide for the congregational respite program. If you come across ideas or methods of working in this area of study, please let us know, as we are constantly struggling to make our program the best that it can be. Always remember that we are all called to work as unto the Lord and in so doing we will give Him the glory and honor for all that we do. In the name of the Father, the Son, and the Holy Spirit we pray. Amen.

Reverend Sheri Smith
Minister of Congregational Care
First United Methodist Church
Lawrenceville, Georgia

The Caregiver

As I watch you fall into memories
Of oh - so long ago…
My face becomes a stranger-
One you no longer know.

Often there are good days and
We sit and talk as friends.
My loneliness and bitterness
Are like they'd never been.

But all too soon you turn away-
Push aside my caring hands…
I'm left to love for the both of us-
Making futile, empty plans.

So each morning as I talk with God,
And we share our love for you…
He gives me strength as I speak your name
And I pray you'll know me too.

Jane Johnson

Table of Contents

Introduction

Whether you are considering starting a congregational respite program or have already made the commitment to begin one, I hope and pray that this manual will aid you in exploring, developing, and launching a ministry at your church that addresses the needs of memory-impaired older adults. These types of programs have the potential to impact many lives. This manual is the result of over three years of developing and fine tuning a congregational respite program at the First United Methodist Church in Lawrenceville, Georgia. Our program is called Grace Arbor, a place where we all "walk with grace".

Grace Arbor was the vision of a group of church members who had the need for respite care for their memory-impaired loved ones. This may be a need you are responding to at your church. The program here required more than four years of persistent inquiry and planning by the church before they were ready to develop it, launch it, and then direct it.

It was during this time that God was preparing me for such a work. After a move from one state to another, I trained to become a Stephen Minister and served in 2 Atlanta area hospitals on their pastoral care teams. My mom developed brain cancer during this time, and dementia became a part of my personal life experience. I saw personally how much respite care impacted my dad. Then my husband experienced cancer, and God taught me about being a caregiver. So many life experiences prepared me for the ministry of Grace Arbor with God orchestrating them for my good and His glory. After Mom's death and my husband's recovery, I felt a restlessness in my spirit. I knew that God was preparing me for a new ministry.

When I saw the ad in the paper about the church starting a day program, it took the encouragement of my family for me to answer it. For me, this is where Proverbs 3:5-6 came to life: ***"Trust in the Lord with all your heart and lean not on your own understanding; in all ways acknowledge Him, and He will make your paths straight."*** I committed the plan of an older adult program, a congregational respite program, to Him. I asked Him to use me and to provide for all of the needs of this program. Over and over, He directed me to necessary resources and even to how we came to name this program Grace Arbor. This ministry and my service continue to be His work and to His glory!

My prayer for you is that you will take the time to read carefully through the chapters. As you read them, keep a pencil and notebook handy to jot down ideas and needs you think of as the Holy Spirit prompts you. I have tried to think of as many details as I could to aid you in creating a quality, Spirit-filled program that will minister to families in crisis and that would impact memory-impaired older adults. Check out the RESOURCE GUIDE at the end of the book for aids to assist you with ideas, equipment, and support.

In addition to praying as I prepared to lead this program, I read as many resources that I could to help me in preparing to lead this ministry. You will want to take advantage of training offered by your local chapter of the Alzheimer's Association. Check out local colleges in your area for any courses that you might take, or possibly audit, to equip you further. Go to Beachwood, Ohio, and be trained in the *Montessori Method for Dementia Patients* through the Myers Research Group. Research the Internet for any training programs coming your way through your local Senior Services or Division of Aging. Keep seeking and the Lord will overwhelm you with the resources to help you in the planning, implementation, and running of your program.

Chapter 1

Getting Started

Apple Pie Day

Starting a Congregational Respite program is one of the greatest spiritual adventures a church can undertake to do. The opportunities to impact families in a time of crisis are monumental, as are opportunities for church and community members to utilize their gifts and talents. Memory impairment in older adults is on the increase; statistics from the Alzheimer's Association are staggering. At present, over five million people have been diagnosed with Alzheimer's disease. By 2050 the number is estimated to increase to sixteen million. This population needs support and assistance. I believe that it can be the church's mission to accomplish this.

The greatest work a church can do as it considers opening a Congregational Respite program is to pray. Our Lord and Savior promised the Holy Spirit to all who seek Him. Under His direction, you will be able to perform an amazing, fruit-bearing ministry; apart from Him, you won't. As you begin, I would encourage a team of people who have a heart for this ministry to pray and seek God for a period of time, i.e., taking a month to write down what the Lord might reveal to each as they pray. After the time is up, gather together and have each person share what the Lord has shown to them. I believe that you will then have the beginning of your ministry.

I would seek wise counsel. Talk to people in the community about needs. Talk to doctors, to county senior organizations, and to the local chapter of the Alzheimer's Association about the

1

number of calls they are getting for help. As you poll Sunday school classes in various churches, target, not only older adult classes, but mid-age classes as well. They, too, might be the caregivers to aging parents or grandparents. The needs in your church and community will make themselves known.

As you seek wise counsel, you will need to prepare a financial plan to pay for this ministry. Will this come about as a "line item" in the church budget? Perhaps a gift or memorial might be the financial springboard to get it going. You might consider applying for a grant. Whichever route you choose, you will need money in hand to purchase equipment, to modify an existing space or to build a new space to house this ministry, and to pay salaries for the staff who will be required to implement, launch, and direct this program.

Another important component to this process is researching your state and local laws concerning respite programs. Are programs like these licensed by the state in which your church is located? If not, what are the guidelines, rules, and regulations you must follow in order *not* to be licensed? In the state of Georgia, a group of Congregational Respite Program directors worked diligently with state legislators to prevent these programs from being licensed.

As you go through this process, contact existing programs in other communities, as well as the Alzheimer's Association, for help with training and for help with training and "shadowing". These visits and training will prove invaluable as you plan this ministry for your church. These people will be able to assist you with any guidelines that your state might require for a program such as this. Your Area Agency on Aging will be able to answer many questions for you.

The more you plan on the front end, the fewer opportunities exist for "surprises" to occur after you are well on your way to starting your program. Praying, seeking wise counsel, putting together a financial plan, and looking into state laws will aid you in putting together a plan. Shadowing existing programs and seeking support from the Alzheimer's Association will help to fine tune that plan. Now you are ready to fine tune even further by looking at your space, purchasing equipment and supplies, and getting your paperwork in order.

Notes:

Chapter 2

Equipment and Supplies

St Patrick's Day Table Decor

The term *equipment* encompasses non-consumable items that are used on a daily basis. These include chairs, tables, coffeepots, dishes, etc. An assessment of what your church presently has in the way of equipment will be helpful in reducing this component of your budget. Asking church members for donations will also be helpful. Don't be afraid to refuse any item that will not fit your needs. If you don't need an item, it is better to say *no* than to take up storage space with something you won't use.

Following is a list of necessary items. From my experience, each item on this list will help you as you creatively plan your program. Some things, such as mixers or blenders, will not be needed until you do a cooking project; others you will need right away. The Internet is a valuable tool to use as you search for these items. Comparison shop! Don't be afraid to ask for discounts or donations from a company. Asking for a discount price because you are starting a respite ministry might generate some additional equipment.

Necessary Equipment

1. Sturdy arm chairs that can be stacked for storage
2. Washable cushions for arm chairs
3. Tables for eating and doing activities
4. Dishes: mugs, glasses, plates (luncheon and dessert), bowls, silverware, pitchers for drinks, cream and sugar containers, serving bowls, casseroles and serving utensils for lunch and cooking projects, cookie sheets.* If you have a working kitchen in your church that is being used for Wednesday night dinners, some of these items may possibly be borrowed on a regular basis.
5. Two 36-cup coffeepots - one for coffee and one for hot water (for tea and hot chocolate)
6. Microwave for heating and cooking projects
7. Toaster oven or full-sized oven
8. Electric mixer
9. Blender
10. Cloth tablecloths - solid or checked
11. Sing-along books (large print)
12. Hymnals (large print)
13. Storage units - cupboards with counter tops
14. Working sink with running hot and cold water
15. Cloth hand towels
16. Nametags - clear plastic holder with clip, not pin
17. Name place cards for the table with holders
18. Placemats that can be wiped clean
19. Decorating items - quilts for the walls, pictures, flower vases, silk flower arrangements for the tables when fresh flowers aren't available, seasonal décor, such as Christmas tree and unbreakable ornaments
20. Aprons and plastic gloves for crafts
21. CD player
22. Exercise Equipment: balls (yoga, small balls, nerf balls), exercise bands, one-pound bags of beans, plastic basketball goal, net for balloon volleyball, balloons, bean bags
23. White board and markers/eraser for daily schedule
24. First Aid Kit
25. Telephone
26. File Cabinet
27. Computer w/printer
28. Yearly calendar
29. Accordion file with manila folders for participant records
30. Digital camera
31. Baskets for transporting things
32. Extra wheelchairs and walker
33. Extra sweaters or sweatshirts
34. Piano or keyboard
35. Sleeping bag or cot for emergencies

Chairs are one of the most important pieces of equipment you will purchase. When shopping for chairs, look for sturdy, high-backed ones that can be wiped clean. Accidents will occur, so look for chairs that can be totally wiped down and sanitized. A cloth-covered chair would not work in this ministry. I found that the Grosiflex Pacific Fanback stacking armchair met our needs perfectly. It has held up well and has been easy to move, to keep clean and sanitized. It is stackable and comes in a variety of colors. We went with a bronze color which is easily seen and goes with all décor. For comfort, we use cloth-stuffed cushions from various stores that can be spot cleaned, sprayed with sanitizing spray, or thrown in the wash. Keeping cost at $4 a cushion by purchasing on sale or at discount stores helps plan for future replacement costs.

When I started Grace Arbor, we had bulky old tables. We made do with these until the ministry could afford to purchase replacements. I have since replaced these tables with the white plastic ones you can buy at the different discount stores. They come in various sizes. I have 8-foot, 4-foot, and round tables in the program. The 4-foot table makes a nice "communion" table when draped with a white cloth. The fact that they are plastic makes them easy to move and wipe clean after projects. They are stackable as well for ease in storage.

Dishes were an important investment as I wanted to create a friendly atmosphere of "home" that would spark fellowship and conversation. We do not eat on paper plates with plastic utensils at home nor do we drink from Styrofoam cups. I considered safety a big factor, especially with cups and mugs. Were they easily tipped? Were they too heavy for older arthritic hands to pick up? Were they cost-effective? Were they environmentally friendly? Could they be easily cleaned and sanitized? I have bought white mugs, plates, and bowls. Food can easily be seen on white. I offer these words of caution, however: don't put a white plate, mug, or bowl on a white placemat. White on white or any of the same color on the same color can be "lost" visually to someone with memory impairment

I decided cloth tablecloths were better than vinyl. They were tactilely more appealing and would last longer. Additionally, they added to that homey atmosphere. I have found the less busy the pattern the better the impact on the table. (See example in picture.) I have several colors that can be used for different seasons. For example, red and white check can be used in February, July, and December, and on Memorial Day and Veteran's Day. I have laminated construction paper for placemats. Some are plain, but most are in designs that a volunteer created. These are seasonal with matching name place cards

I use colorful, seasonal cocktail napkins that go with placemats for morning snack, adding again to that homey atmosphere. Anything that is visually appealing is important. I may just use solid-colored or find print ones. *One way to get these is to advertise in the church bulletin for members to donate cocktail napkins!* You will be amazed at the results. I use white paper napkins for lunch with the exception of birthdays and holidays.

I am not a fan of silk flowers; they, however, are useful on the lunch and snack table if fresh ones are not available. Ask anyone in the church during flower-growing season if they would bring flowers on a weekly basis for your tables. You can also decorate tables with seasonal fruit and vegetables. Anything that will stimulate conversation is great!

My hymnals and sing-along books are 1 1/2" binders with plastic sleeves. In the sleeves, are the words in large print - Arial 20 or larger. In the sing-along books, there are dividers which are color-coded for easy identifying. The pages are numbered in each section. Example – Patriotic section page 3 would be labeled as P3. I have binders with just Christmas music, both sacred and secular. The binders are 1 1/2 inches so they won't be too heavy.

Nametags and place cards at the table are important for several reasons. Memory-impaired adults have a hard time remembering names. Until you and your volunteers get to know everyone well, *you will forget their names, too*! Nametags solve that dilemma. Reusable nametags that clip on or pin on will work well. On the nametag, print the participant's name in a large Arial font in a color that is different from that of your volunteers'. I use purple for participants and black for volunteers. These colors are close enough to distinguish between but not glaringly obvious that they are different. This is an issue to address to make the participants feel *part* of the ministry - actively involved - not set apart because they are being cared for in your program. Your nametags will serve as a safety feature as well. Somewhere on the tag - front or back - identify your program in case a participant wanders off and is found by someone. Your nametags can also have identifying marks that tell your volunteers that a person is a diabetic. We use a red heart to identify our diabetics.

Place cards at the table will allow for targeted placement of your participants. You will be able to control where they sit and by whom. I try to mix volunteers in between participants as much as possible to keep the conversation flowing. Volunteer placement can aid in personality conflicts between participants. On the place card, as on the nametag, a red heart will be found if someone is a diabetic.

Supplies

Supplies are the consumable things that are used on a daily, weekly, or monthly basis. These will be replaced as needed. These things could be identified for your church's congregation as items to be donated. Suggest when someone shops that they pick up a box of decaf tea or hot chocolate. You will need to be specific about brand names and quantities!

1. Decaffeinated coffee, decaffeinated tea bags - both individual and family size, hot chocolate-plain, no sugar-added, and diet - lemonade (sugar free)
2. Sugar, Splenda, coffee creamer, whipped cream (for hot chocolate)
3. Paper products - paper plates for crafts as well as desserts or snacks when you don't want to use china - paper towels, napkins, both cocktail and luncheon, and paper towels
4. Clear plastic service gloves for serving food and doing crafts
5. Condiments for meals and snacks
6. Sanitizing wipes (whatever is on sale)
7. Dishwasher detergent/sponges
8. Lysol or other disinfecting spray
9. Depends disposable undergarments
10. Gloves - latex or non latex - exam gloves for emergencies

Notes:

Chapter 3

Staffing

In this section I will discuss staff, both paid and volunteer. Without a staff that is godly, Spirit-empowered, and with a heart for this kind of ministry, you will fail. Your staff is vital to this ministry on many levels. It is your staff who will be assisting you in ministry to your participants and programming functions. They will be your prayer partners, advocates, servants, and advertisers. If they have a heart for this ministry and feel validated and appreciated, they will do just about anything for you because they believe in what they do. I cannot say enough about how important both the paid and volunteer staff are.

As I began to plan Grace Arbor, I did several things to advertise the need for help. At that time, I was the only paid staff. I knew that I needed a group of people who would commit to one day or part of a day on a weekly basis. I also needed people who would be willing to substitute for the regular volunteers. The first thing I did was to pray. I asked the Lord to move in the hearts of those who had hearts for this type of ministry. I prayed for volunteers who loved older people and who weren't afraid of interacting with people who are memory-impaired.

After I prayed, I began to advertise in our church's bulletin and its monthly newsletter. I tried to include both eye-catching and heart-catching ads about the needs of this ministry. Then I began to meet people and to share personally about this ministry. I spoke in church services and visited Sunday school classes. I even put an ad in out Parent Morning Out and the Preschool's newsletters, hoping some moms who had time on their hands might be willing to help. I asked around, and people gave me names of people I personally contacted.

As I interviewed each potential "staff" member, I asked them to share with me why they wanted to volunteer and what experiences they had had with people with memory impairment. Most of my volunteers have had a family member, a neighbor, or a friend who suffered with dementia. If someone were too "close" to the situation, I asked that they wait or serve in another way that didn't involve immediate contact with persons with dementia. I learned early on that these questions are important. I had recruited a volunteer who was helping with food because her parents had recently died from dementia. I felt as though she didn't need to be in too close contact with our participants. The situation went from bad to worse, and we both realized at about the same time that she had not given herself sufficient time to grieve. She dropped out of the staff pool at about the time that I was going to ask her to leave.

We are committed to providing the best quality care we can for our caregivers. This is why we conduct a background check on all staff, both paid and volunteer. This has been an added cost to our budget, but it has been well worth it in the confidence we portray to our caregivers. At this time, I am also requiring a TB test for all staff. This is another added assurance for caregivers.

God is so faithful. At the time when we needed volunteers, He assembled a mighty group of men and women who were committed to serving in the areas of their gifts and talents. My promise to them was that I would provide the training to equip them to do what I asked them to do. I have kept that commitment by having quarterly trainings to empower each volunteer concerning behaviors, about elderly abuse, and about safety issues. I asked our local chapter of the Alzheimer's Association to assist in those trainings initially until I felt comfortable enough to do them on my own.

As our program has grown, we have added paid staff. I now have an (almost) fulltime Assistant Director , a very part-time administrative assistant, and part-time cook who handles meals and snacks. Each addition has brought blessings and challenges. The blessings are sharing in the ministry and its precious people we serve. The challenges are to train and support paid staff while directing a fulltime ministry that serves caregivers, participants, and volunteers. I juggle many balls, and without the Holy Spirit and a loving, supportive family, I would be failing at what I do.

As I recruited paid staff, the same philosophy applied: I looked for people who have a heart for this ministry and who have had experience working with memory-impaired older adults. This work is not for everyone.

When I interviewed for my Assistant Director's job, I looked for high-energy, social people who were qualified in certain ways. It was not quick work, and I interviewed many people. My requirement before I hire either volunteers or paid staff is that they come and spend a day at Grace Arbor. You learn a lot about people as you observe them in action. For the paid staff, I might have them spend a week shadowing me. It is necessary for people to experience this type of ministry firsthand. Many may have a preconceived idea of what it looks like. Unless they are there, hands-on, they will never know what it is really like to work in that environment.

My Assistant Director must be certified in Alzheimer's care. This is a 22-hour program offered by the Alzheimer's Association. The daily workshops cover a lot of ground. This program is a tool that is important in the overall plan of the ministry. My Assistant Director must also be CPR and First Aid-trained. Both of these trainings will prepare him or her to step into my shoes if I have to be out for any reason. I would try to set my schedule so that I would not be away during the first three months of training. As he or she gains confidence, I will gradually let him or her be "in charge" while I am present. This helps me to share expectations after the day is over, affirming and guiding him or her to that place of confidence.

As I began to interview people for the Assistant Director's job, I heard a spot on the radio about singer Wayne Newton. He was being interviewed about some of the people on his show and how talented they were. The interviewer asked him if he were worried that someone would get so good that he, Wayne Newton, would be out of a job.

Mr. Newton replied that he felt it was his job to support and help his singers become the very best they could be, even if he risked losing them. When I heard that, I thought *That is what I want to do!* I want to help people to achieve to the greatest of their potential. If I can do that, I have done my best.

Notes:

Chapter 4

Training

Volunteer Training

As I mentioned in the previous section, I made a covenant with my volunteers concerning training. I feel that it is my job as director to help my staff, both volunteer and paid, to be the best they can be as they serve these precious participants. The more people are educated and gain knowledge concerning a particular subject, the better able they are to be prepared to apply that knowledge to any given situation. The more my staff knows about dementia - its behaviors, the triggers that cause behavior, and how to react in certain situations - the better our program will run. Instead of my rushing to put out fires, my staff will be dousing them before they get started with their loving knowledge, which translates into caring behavior. I can't say enough about the importance of good training.

One aspect of training I find extremely helpful in working with people with dementia is for our staff to be able to role play. As we learn about a behavior and its triggers, we will role play what that might look like. Each day has so many examples, as well. I will try to bring up examples of situations they have experienced, and we will brainstorm how to handle them: what might work and what won't normally work. Spot training is also very effective. If a challenging situation presents itself, it is an opportunity for a learning experience. At the end of the day and subsequent days, I will cover with all volunteers what happened, how it was handled, and what

9

we could possibly have done differently. I engage my volunteers for their opinion, but I am ultimately the decision maker.

Here are some ideas from past trainings I have done that will equip you as you start and sustain your program:

1. General Overview of Dementia
2. Behaviors - What to Expect
3. Behavioral Triggers - the How's and Why's and How to Respond
4. Elder Abuse
5. Participants' Rights
6. Brief Overview of Montessori Method
7. Safety: Universal Precautions
8. CPR/ First Aid training
9. Role Playing

Notes:

Volunteer Training
Role Playing

The following situations can be used in a training class where volunteers pair up, discuss the scenario with their solution, and then discuss as a group. Each situation can be adapted to actual situations you have dealt with in your program.

Situation 1:
You are sitting in the chair circle - morning or afternoon group time - and the participant next to you suddenly gets up and walks to the door. What will you do?

Situation 2:
You are sitting next to someone at the lunch table who is not eating at all. What will you do?

Situation 3:
You are sitting at the lunch table, and Robin gives the invitation to come and do an activity. The participant next to you says, "I don't want to do that." What will you do?

Situation 4:
You are sitting in group and two participants sitting near you get into a verbal sparring match. What will you do?

Situation 5:
As you are sitting in the group, you notice one of the participants become glassy-eyed and rigid in body posturing. What will you do?

Situation 6:
You are in the bathroom with a participant, and she bangs her elbow on the stall door, and it begins to bleed. What will you do?

Situation 7:
Robin is leading devotional, and the participant next to you is talking to another participant rather than paying attention. What will you do?

Situation 8:
You and a participant are having a conversation about life, and the participant shares an elaborate story about his or her past. What will you do?

Chapter 5

Paperwork, i.e., Forms and Documents

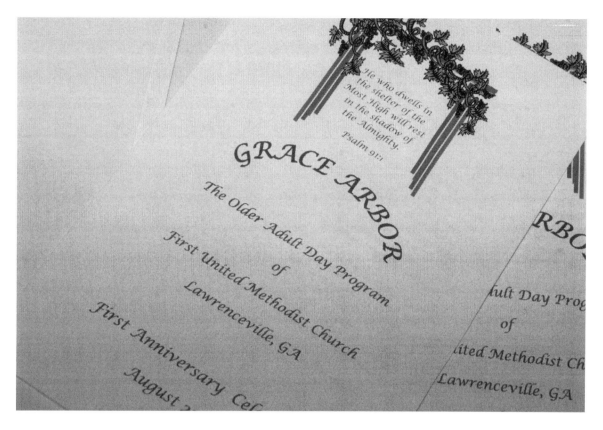

Grace Arbor Brochure

Paperwork, i.e., forms and documents, are the record of what you do on a daily basis. The more organized you can be in your paperwork, the easier your job will be as you go through your day. As I go through this section, I will give examples of the forms I use. You will need to change them to fit your specific needs. I will split this into several sections that will explain the type of form, why you need it, and what it does for you in your record keeping.

1. Potential Participant Folder with Documents
   a. Letter from Pastor
   b. Bylaws and Procedures
   c. Medical Release
   d. Emergency Release
   e. Photo and Field Trip Releases
   f. Participant Information Sheets
   g. Business Card with Grace Arbor's contact information
   h. Brochure about Grace Arbor
   i. Current newsletter
   j. Medical Release

      k. T.B. Results

      l. Emergency Release

      m. Photo and Field Trip Releases

      n. Participant Information Sheets

      o. Current Photo

      p. DNR, living will, and durable power of attorney forms for those in hospice care.

      q. Drug Information Sheet with current prescriptions, if separate from info sheet

2. Participant File (*Keep this in Program Room at all times in Accordion File!*)

3. Volunteer Folder with documents

      r. Reducing the Risk Background Check

      s. Information Sheet w/Emergency Contact

      t. Covenant

4. Attendance Roll

5. Telephone Call Sheet

6. Safety Forms

      u. Fire Drill Report

      v. Participant Accident Form

      w. Volunteer Accident Form

7. Calendar

8. Caregiver Monthly Newsletter

9. Volunteer Monthly Newsletter

10.. 911 Call Sheet

11. Emergency Activity Folder

12. Participant Notebook

13. Brochure and Business Cards

1. Potential Participant Folder with Documents

    This is what I hand to a caregiver after we have determined together that the loved one will be a part of the Grace Arbor ministry. I use two-pocket folders in particular colors. For my benefit, because our logo is purple and teal, my participant folder is purple and my volunteer folder is teal. This is a quick, visual determinant for me as I keep my folders on the same shelf!

    It was decided that a ***letter from our pastor*** was an added assurance to the caregiver that our church and our pastor are behind this ministry 100%.

    The most time-consuming piece of paper for you will be the creation of your ***bylaws and policies and procedures sheets***. These will give the caregivers the assurance that you have policies and procedures in place for the safety of their loved one. These documents will be developed as you and your committee decide what to do when you take someone from "intake" to leaving the program permanently. These lay out the structure of your program and how you will do what you say you will do.

    The ***medical release form*** is one the caregiver gives to the doctor to fill out to say that this potential participant is physically able to participate in our program.

    The ***emergency release form*** will give us permission to care for and get care for this participant in the event of an emergency. This directs the ambulance to the hospital of choice in case we have to call 911.

The ***photo and field trip release forms*** are self explanatory. If you take pictures or have an event printed in the newspaper, this is nice to have on hand.

The ***information sheet*** includes vital questions about this person's past, their former life prior to memory loss, and what they can do now. This also has a place for contact info. I can't stress enough the importance of having all contact numbers in case of an emergency.

It is just as important for the caregiver to be able to reach me. I put two numbers on my ***business card*** - the church's number and the cell# to reach Grace Arbor.

I include a brochure in this folder. It briefly spells out our program and the fees. This is easier to read through than the policy and procedures. It is also there to be passed on to someone else, should there be other interest in our program.

A ***monthly newsletter*** contains current information and that month's schedule of activities.

2. Participant File* *Keep this in Program Room at all times in an Accordion File.**

I keep an accordion file with all of my current participant folders with me at all times during the operating day of Grace Arbor. If we have a fire drill, it goes outside with me. I guard this with my life because it contains all the forms the participant's caregiver filled out. In addition to the ***completed medical forms*** they filled out, I keep their current ***TB test results***, a ***current photo,*** and any additional information the family might give me. I have for those in hospice care, ***DNR, living will, and durable power of attorney forms. Current prescriptions*** may be found in this file, as well. I lock this file up each night.

3. Volunteer Folder with documents

As I mentioned earlier, this folder is a different color from the participant's folder. Our church has a policy which I think should pertain to any care-giving ministry. It is that all care-giving ministry volunteers must have a background check. We use the local police department. There is a fee for this, but it is well worth it in the long run. My volunteers also fill out a covenant in which they agree to certain things, and I agree to certain things. They then sign and date this.

4. Attendance Roll

This sheet is set up to track the daily attendance of participants as well as to serve as a financial sheet at the end of the month. I document the number of meals served to participants, volunteers, and staff.

5. Telephone Call Sheet

I use this sheet to take down information from phone calls concerning interest in our ministry. I will keep this in a folder to refer to if the caregiver isn't yet ready to visit. When I receive the next call from that caregiver, I have additional information to use in talking with him or her. This also a great way to track the number of calls you receive in a month.

6. Safety Forms

Safety forms need to be on hand at all times, and *fire drills* need to be documented. These should be done at least quarterly, on different days with different volunteers present. These drills help to prepare your program staff in case of a real emergency. Tornado drills would be extremely important, especially if you live in Tornado Alley.

Accident forms must be completed every time there is an incident requiring more than minor care (ex. bumping thin skin which would call for cleansing and a Band-Aid versus a fall that would require more attention.) These forms should be filled out when this happens to anyone in the program area. These forms must be signed by caregiver as documentation that they have been made aware of an accident and what kind of care was given. These signed forms need to be retained in the participants' folders as part of their permanent records. *Volunteer Accidents* should also be documented.

7. Calendar

A notebook type of calendar will be extremely beneficial to you in all areas of your work as director of your program. I use an 18- month calendar which allows caregivers and volunteers to "sign out" when they aren't coming to Grace Arbor. I plan my attendance for the week in my calendar and then check it against true attendance. This helps me to plan for additional volunteers and meals. I record meetings and anything else I need to keep track of by date. It is helpful for all staff members to have one and to compare notes frequently in order to stay on track as a team.

I keep another type of a calendar for my activities, and I use it in monthly planning. I keep a copy of it in my file cabinet under that particular month's folder. I keep files on different seasonal activities adjacent to those monthly folders so they are easily referred to as needed for planning.

8. Caregiver Monthly Newsletter

Every month I create a newsletter for both my caregivers and volunteers. In it I include a schedule of special activities we will do during that month. I might highlight special clothing needs pertaining to that activity. For example, if we are painting birdhouses on a certain day, I will ask them to wear old clothes. The challenge will be whether the caregiver keeps the calendar and refers to it frequently during the month. I communicate support group meetings and any information that needs to be relayed in the newsletters, and I list birthdays for that month.

9. Volunteer Monthly Newsletter

As in the caregiver newsletter, I include a schedule of specific events happening during the month, including birthdays. I will communicate any issues that might have come up during the month to help in their ongoing training. Both the volunteer and the caregiver newsletters are important documents. I keep them in a file on my computer.

10. 911 Call Sheet

This is a set of instructions that anyone can use when calling 911 for our program. It contains our address and phone number and specific directions to our program room. In an emergency situation, volunteers may not be able to think as clearly as they would under normal circumstances. This is an aid to give them the support they need in a crisis.

11. Emergency Activity Folder

This folder is vitally important to those who are assisting you in your program. If there is an emergency, this folder will equip a volunteer to do an activity with the remaining participants while the director and emergency personnel render aid. This folder should be easily accessible and full of different ideas depending on the time of day and the area of the room in which the crisis has occurred.

12. Participant Notebook

This is a binder containing a sheet on each active participant in your program. Each sheet should include a picture and general information about the person. This binder helps volunteers to become familiar with new participants. It takes time to keep current, but it is invaluable! It assists volunteers by listing pertinent information about each participant to aid them in conversation topics. For example, "Sue," a new participant, was a WWII pilot who flew in active duty. As a volunteer, I can generate conversation topics around those experiences, also engaging others who may also have served in WWII.

13 Brochure and Business Cards

Nothing speaks "professional" like a well-designed brochure and business cards. Your brochure could be the first impression a stranger will have as they learn about your program. A brochure should contain this pertinent information:

1. Your mission statement
2. Your staff
3. The program's daily schedule
4. Activities - the particulars
5. Contact information for additional questions.

Notes:

The Congregational Respite Program of
First United Methodist Church of Lawrenceville

Application Form

Full Name: _____Date:_____Fee Paid:_____

Address:_____

Male__ Female__ Birthday_____ Marital Status: Married__Single__Divorced__Widow/er__

Presently lives with_____

How did you hear about our program? _____

EMERGENCY INFORMATION:

Doctor's Name _____

Address _____Phone #_____

Hospital Preference: _____

ALLERGIC TO: _____

List all physical problems, including mental health issues and communicable diseases.

_____

_____

List any dietary or physical restrictions.

_____

_____

List medications/dosage:_____

_____

Caregiver Contact Information:

Caregiver's Name: _____ Relationship_____

Address if different from participant: _____

Phone Numbers:
(H)_____(C)_____(W)_____

Alternate Contact Person: _____ Relationship_____

Address_____

Phone Numbers: (H) _____ (C)_____(W)_____

(Use back for any additional information we may need to know to aid in the participant's care.)

I, _____, have received and read a copy of the policies and procedures of

Grace Arbor. DATE: _____

GRACE ARBOR

Interest Profile

Name: _____ Date: _____

Name Participant likes to be called: _____

Family History (marital history, number and names of children, where they live, and other important relationships:

_____

_____

_____

Friends/Pets:_____

_____

Childhood History (Place of birth, info on parents, nationality, languages spoken, experiences, passtimes):

_____

_____

_____

Education/Former Occupations (Years of work, what they enjoyed):

_____

_____

Previous interests, Awards, Volunteer Activities: _____

_____

Current Interests and Hobbies: _____

_____

Musical Tastes (Play instrument? Sing? What music do they enjoy?):

_____

Clubs/Organizations: _____

Religious Preference: _____

Social Interaction (Enjoy large social functions? Small groups? Being alone?)

_____

_____

Comments: _____

_____

_____

_____

GRACE ARBOR

Photo and Field Trip Release

Name: _____ Date: _____

The above-mentioned named participant gives permission and release for **Photographs** to be made of him/ her while engaged in program activities. These photos may be used for publicity/promotion of Grace Arbor and also for identification purposes.

Participant_____ Guardian_____

The above-named participant gives permission and release to participate in **Field Trips and Outings** by Grace Arbor. Every effort will be made to insure the safety of the participant.

Participant _____ Guardian _____

STATEMENT OF MEDICAL CONDITION

Date:_____

Dear Physician:

    This patient has applied to attend ***Grace Arbor, the Congregational Respite Program of First United Methodist Church.*** Please certify that he/she is free of communicable diseases and has had the necessary and appropriate immunizations.

Name_____Birthdate_____

Address_____City/StateZip_____

Diagnosis_____

Date of last: Flu shot_____Pneumonia vaccine_____

Tetanus Toxoid_____TB test_____

Results were positive _____negative_____

Allergies: _____
Please circle the recommended diet for this patient:

Regular   Low Salt   Low Cholesterol   Diabetic/low calorie

    Other_____

Special considerations/precautions/comments:_____
_____

I certify that the above-named patient is free of communicable diseases and recommend his/her participation in the Grace Arbor Congregational Respite Program.

Signature_____Date_____

Address_____

                                         Respectfully,

                                    _____

                                    Robin Dill, Director
                                    Grace Arbor
                                    Congregational Respite Program

GRACE ARBOR

Consent for Emergency Medical Care

As a participant in the Grace Arbor Congregational Respite Program of First United Methodist Church of Lawrenceville, I hereby give permission to staff (paid and volunteers) to provide direct minor emergency care for minor emergencies or to access 911 emergency medical services as deemed necessary. I hereby give my full and unconditional approval for said staff to secure emergency medical care.

Any resultant bill will be the responsibility of the participant and /or caregiver/guardian. Said individual(s) will be responsible for filing any and all medical insurance claims.

In the event a medical situation is not an emergency, staff may request that a doctor see the participant. It is understood that the participant cannot return to the program without a report concerning the incident.

I will not hold any of the staff (paid or volunteer) of Grace Arbor responsible for any injury, which occurs to the named participant during the course of the program. I acknowledge that Grace Arbor cannot and does not assume responsibility for undesirable incidents or injuries should the participant leave the program site without permission.

Every reasonable effort will be made to ensure the safety of the participant.

Name: _____ Date: _____

Guardian (relationship)_____ Date: _____

Signature: _____

Participant's Physician Name and Phone #:
_____

Hospital of Choice: _____

Participants' Rights

1. The right to be treated as an adult, with respect and dignity.
2. The right to participate in a program of services and activities that promotes positive attitudes on one's usefulness and capabilities.
3. The right to be free from physical, mental, sexual, and verbal abuse, neglect, and exploitation.
4. The right to be free from actual or threatened physical or chemical restraints.
5. The right to be encouraged and supported in maintaining one's independence to the extent that conditions and circumstances permit, and to be involved in a program of services designed to promote personal independence.
6. The right to self-determination within the respite setting, including the opportunity to decide whether or not to participate in any given activity; be involved to the extent possible in program planning and operation; to refuse to participate in activities; the right to be cared about in an atmosphere of sincere interest and concern in which needed support and services are provided.
7. The right to privacy and confidentiality.
8. The right to be made aware of the grievance process.

GRACE ARBOR
The Congregational Respite Program of
First United Methodist Church of Lawrenceville
395 West Crogan Street
Lawrenceville, GA 30045
770-973-0386 – Ext. 126
Cell: 678-758-3554

POLICIES AND PROCEDURES MANUAL

Governing Body

The Congregational Respite Program is a ministry of the Health & Wholeness and Congregational Care Committees of First United Methodist Church of Lawrenceville.

Purpose

Grace Arbor is designed to meet the social and emotional needs of older adults and their caregivers. It provides activities and socialization opportunities outside the home in a safe and caring setting for older adults with mild to moderate memory loss and/or medical impairments. It provides their caregivers with emotional support through a caregiver support group, information regarding available resources, and personal time away during the day in which to rest and address their own needs.

Services Offered

For the Older Adult Participant:

This ministry provides a safe, loving environment for the well-being of each participant. A variety of activities includes, but is not limited to, social, creative, intellectual, spiritual, and recreational programming. All activities are designed to provide mental stimulation and social participation. Examples of activities include group singing, gardening, crafts, community services, reminiscing, exercise, adapted floor games, intergenerational programs, art therapy, pet therapy, and socialization activities.

For the Caregiver:

This ministry provides respite (an interval of rest or relief) for the caregiver. It supports the efforts of the family to keep the loved one in the home environment, which will contribute to the quality of life of the participant as well as the family. This ministry offers a bi-monthly support group with an experienced counselor. It also provides information regarding available community resources, nursing home options, Alzheimer information, etc.

Hours, Days of Operation, Location

Grace Arbor Program operates on Mondays, Tuesdays, Thursdays and Fridays from 10:00 a.m. to 3:00 p.m. in the G-36 area of the church. The program will be closed on all legal holidays, i.e., New Year's Day, Martin Luther King Day, Memorial Day, Fourth of July, Labor Day, Thanksgiving Day and Christmas Day, if they fall on a normal program day, and other holidays

that fall on program days. Advanced notification of closing will be communicated to participants and caregivers. If the Gwinnett county schools are closed for inclement weather, we will also be closed.

Admission Criteria

Participation in the program will be based on the applicant's ability to participate in the program and the initial interview with the director. Taken into consideration when evaluating whether an applicant is capable of participating in the program are the following:

- Medical stability – A participant may be frail and have physical problems, but must be medically stable.
- Ability to ambulate independently with or without assistive devices without potential danger to self or others
- Ability to perform daily living activities independently
- Ability to interact and socialize with others
- Ability to exhibit acceptable behavior in a group

The following may be examples for excluding an applicant from Grace Arbor:

- Unmanaged incontinence
- Disruptive or combative behavior
- Psychosis
- Communicable disease
- Need for one-on-one continual supervision

Admission Procedure

1. A telephone interview will be conducted by the director, followed by (if potential participant meets criteria) an invitation to visit the program for a day with the participant and caregiver attending. Following assessment an application will be given to the caregiver to be returned to the director.

2. The Admission application is processed and the applicant and family are informed of the decision.

3. The participant/family completes the enrollment form, and a registration fee ($40) is paid.

Discharge/Termination Criteria

Examples of reasons for discharging a participant from the program are the same as those listed under Admission Criteria (examples for excluding an applicant section).

If the caregiver is no longer satisfied with our program or a participant is no longer able to take part in the program due to physical or mental deterioration, the director reserves the right to discontinue the participant from the program. The caregiver will be contacted by phone, e-mail, or in person about the need for discharge of the participant. At this time, the director will provide the family with suggestions of program options in the Gwinnett County

area that may better serve their needs. Successful placement is not the responsibility of the staff of Grace Arbor.

Discharge/Termination Procedure

Consideration of discharge from the program will be discussed with the family member(s) before final decision of termination is made in order to give as much advance notice as is reasonably possible. Upon the final decision, that discharge will occur and any daily fees paid in advance will be refunded.

Payments/Rates/Attendance

There is a daily fee of $40 per day for participation in the program which is paid monthly. Statements are issued at the end of the month for the number of days the participant has attended the program. Payment is expected by the 10th of each month in order to ensure uninterrupted participation in the program.

Participants are expected to attend the program as scheduled. Caregivers are asked to notify the director by 9:00 a.m. if the participant will not be in attendance that day. Non-attendance affects both staffing and meal ordering. There is no charge for days not attended; communication to the director or assistant director, however, is vital to day-to-day planning. A $6.50 food service fee will be charged for days the participant is scheduled to attend, does not attend, and does not notify the director or assistant.

Staffing

A director and assistant director will staff the program. The director and assistant director are trained in CPR and first aid. In the director's absence, the assistant director will be in charge of the operation and activities of Grace Arbor. Trained volunteers provide additional staffing and are assigned participants with whom they will socialize during the day. The ratio of volunteers to participants may vary from 2-4 participants to one volunteer, depending upon individuals. Each program day will be considered "full" when it numbers 23.

A mid-morning snack upon arrival, a nutritious lunch, and an early afternoon snack (on an as-needed basis, prior to departure) will be served daily. Beverages such as decaffeinated coffee and tea, water, and juices will be available to participants during the day.

Communication

It is of great importance that lines of communication between caregivers and the program director remain open. If the family of the participant has concerns, observations, and/or suggestions they would like to discuss, they are always encouraged to do so. This can be best accomplished by scheduling an appointment with the director.

Medication/Health/Injury

The director will keep a confidential file for each participant. This file will include the following:

- Admissions application

- Enrollment documents
- Consent for emergency treatment
- Bill of Rights
- Photo release form
- Living Will (if applicable)
- DNR order (if applicable)

Participants needing to take medication(s) during program hours must be able to take it/them independently. Participants must keep the medication with them during the day, as we are unable to store medications. Program staff will remind a participant to take his/her medication; however, they are unable to administer any medications. Family members must take full responsibility for medication administration.

No one on staff is a medical professional. If a participant shows signs of illness or infectious disease, the director will contact the participant's caregiver, advising her/him to pick up the participant. Please keep participant at home if temperature is above normal.

Sickness and accidents resulting in physical injury or suspected physical injury will be reported to the director who will arrange for appropriate medical attention to be obtained. The caregiver of the participant will be immediately notified or emergency actions will be taken. If it is deemed necessary, transportation to the hospital will be obtained by calling 911. An accident report will be filed with the signature of the caregiver.

Paid Attendants

Participants may choose to have their personal paid attendant with them during the program hours. Paid assistants will provide necessary aid to their own client, but will be expected to assist their client in participating in the activities as scheduled. They will also be responsible for payment of their own snacks and meals.

Chapter 6

Interviewing a Prospective Participant's Caregiver

Assistant Director Cindy Leake with Marion

One of the most time-consuming parts of the director's job is the initial interview with a caregiver concerning their loved one and his/her needs. I am going to give you an example of a typical phone call that I receive and how I go through the interview process. As I interview this caregiver, notice the questions that I ask. I want to hear what prompted the caregiver to call me, what the physical and mental abilities are of the loved one, what health issues besides dementia they are dealing with, what their financial need might be, and how I can pray for that caregiver at the close of the conversation. I am a detail person (or try to be!!!). As you interview a caregiver, you must take notes. I have a specific sheet on which I record information that the caregiver gives me about the loved one. I fill that in with the details as much as I can, because after I give my information about the program, the caregiver may decide to get back to me. That might take a day, a month, or even 6 months to a year. If I have a document with their information, I can refer to it when they are ready to visit. If it has been a while, I can ask what has changed since our last conversation. The more detailed you can be, the more professional you come across to the caregiver. I keep all my phone sheets in a folder, recording the date which they called and the date I followed up. Let me say here that the sooner you can follow up, preferably within 24

hours, the better. There may be an extreme need with which you can't help, but you can be a sympathetic ear and a voice used by God to offer comfort and support.

There are many calls you will receive where you cannot help. I try to be sensitive to each need presented but very matter-of-fact about the services we can supply and the condition our participants must be in in order to attend our program. The state of Georgia has specific requirements to allow a program to be called a Congregational Respite program. My participants must be able to meet those requirements in order to be a part of our program. I make this clear in the initial interview with the caregiver. If I become slack in this area, we could be fined or closed down. Although I am matter-of-fact, I am still sensitive and use listening skills to support the caregiver. *I will put in a plug for Stephen Ministry right now*. This training has been invaluable to me as I direct our program. It has given me the tools to lovingly support a caregiver in times of crisis, to listen, to share words of encouragement, to help, and to pray. If I don't supply any other support than prayer, I feel good about the conversation. Do I feel frustrated when I can't help? YES! I try to provide resources and ideas to share about what additional help and support might be available to the caregiver. I direct to web sites and other agencies if I can. But more than anything, I can share Jesus' love and compassion with the caregiver in this season of his or her life. **NEVER** tell a caregiver, or anyone else for that matter, that you **"know what they are going through"**. You don't nor ever will. Each person is a unique individual with unique life circumstances and experiences. You have no idea what his or her level of coping is or how he/she is truly handling the situation that has resulted in a call to you. Your best response is *"How can I help?"*

Read through the following typical conversation I had with a caregiver who had called me. If the caregiver leaves a message, I will start the conversation with, "Hi, my name is Robin Dill, and I direct Grace Arbor. You called earlier today. I am sorry I missed your call. How can I help you?"

This is very short but to the point. I will warn you that these initial calls will take 20-30 minutes. I try to factor that time into my schedule as I return calls. Often I will return calls from home at night, giving me a chance to unwind from the day, to get dinner, and to be refueled to answer calls. The only drawback to calling from home is that you may not have every resource available to share and may have to make a follow up call the next day.

Phone Conversation:

"Hi, this is Robin."

"Hi, Robin, my name is Susan Smith, and I am looking for a day care for my mother. She has recently moved in with me after my dad died. She really can't live alone, so my husband and I moved her up here two months ago from Florida. I thought we would enjoy each other's company and do things together, but she is driving me crazy."

"It sounds like you have had a frustrating time. Susan, I am so sorry about the loss of your dad. Was it sudden?"

"Thanks. He had been sick for a while. He was actually caring for mom, and I think he got burned out. His health declined, and he had a heart attack 2 ½ months ago and died. My sister

lived nearby, so she was there to initially help with mom. She works full time, and it just didn't work."

"Susan, I applaud you for bringing your mom into your home. She is grieving right now and will need lots of support. How old is she and what is her condition? Why was your dad caring for her?"

"Yeah, my husband and I talked about it and felt that it was the right thing to do. I think it is what my dad would have wanted. I don't work, so I was the best choice among me and my siblings. My mom is 85 and has Alzheimer's disease; she was diagnosed 5 years ago. She had been doing okay; she was forgetful but able to get around their little town. Dad had to take the car keys away when she kept getting lost going to the grocery store. I think she just wore him out. He could never leave her alone nor would she let him out of her sight. She went to a program a day or two a week and seemed to enjoy it. I called the Alzheimer's Association, and they referred me to you all."

"Susan, what is your mom's physical condition? What is she capable of doing as far as her activities of daily living? And what is her name?"

"My mom's name is Patsy Johnson. She is in good shape. She loves to walk and listen to music. She watches some TV but gets bored. She wants to be around me all the time. I never can even go to the bathroom without her following me!"

"Is she able to toilet on her own? Also, does she like other people? The reason I ask this is that we have specific requirements for this program. Our participants must be able to ambulate on their own with or without a cane or walker, feed and toilet themselves, and function in a group setting. According to state rules and regulations, if your mom is on medication and if it needs to be taken during our operating hours, then she must be able to take it on her own. We are not allowed to dispense medication. We can prompt her to take it, however."

"Yeah, Mom can do all that. She used to be a social butterfly. She was in several groups and loved people."

"Has your mom attended a church in her lifetime? The reason I ask is that we are a congregational respite program, a ministry of the church, and we do activities that are faith-based."

"Yeah mom grew up in the church, and she and dad were very active in their little church in Florida."

At this point in the conversation, I have established that Susan's mother might fit in well at Grace Arbor. I needed, however, to make clear what we offer and what our fees are.

"Susan, let me tell you about our program and how I go about enrolling someone. As I said before, Grace Arbor is a congregational respite program. We minister to older adults who are memory-impaired. We offer a very interactive day which keeps them mentally, physically,

spiritually, and socially stimulated. We are open from 10AM-3PM on Mondays, Tuesdays, Thursdays, and Fridays. We are closed on major holidays and for the Christmas holidays. We have a social time with a snack in the morning when they come in. This helps the participant to make the transition from home to our program. Following this we move into devotions. During devotional time, we sing and read a devotional booklet I have created. It contains scripture and questions that relate to the topic we will talk about. The questions will be reminiscing or those that are simply pertinent to today. We start and close that time with prayer. After devotions we have our movement time which consists of various arm chair exercises. After movement and blessing of food, we have a bathroom break and lunch. After lunch, depending on the day, we do all kinds of things. Sometimes we have outside entertainment or programs. We might do a craft, play a game, or do a service project. I try to vary our days according to the calendar. **At this point I may give her an example of what we did yesterday or last week.** Most days we end our day with a sing-along. We have fun with that. Many of our folks get up and dance during this time."

"Susan, when someone is interested in our program and I feel that they are a match, I invite the caregiver and the potential participant to visit for the day. It gives you a chance to look our program over, and it gives me a chance to assess your loved one. There is no charge for this visit. If it looks good on both ends, I will give you a folder of forms to fill out. We require a TB test and a statement of medical condition from your doctor. When you turn in the paperwork, there is an application fee of $40. The cost for each day your loved one attends is $40. I bill monthly in arrears so you will receive a bill at the end of the first month she attends. Do you have any questions?"

"How many days can she come?"

She can come all 4 days we are open, or she may attend 3 or 2 or even 1 day per week. You set the schedule. We cannot do a drop-in, however. I submit my food count a week ahead of time, and we shop for supplies in advance. For these reasons, drop-ins are not possible. If things change and you have dr. visits or appointments, you need to let me know. There is no cost for the days she doesn't come; however, if she is sick, I ask that you call me before 9AM to let me know she isn't coming."

"Okay, that sounds good. Do you take Medicare?"

"No, we don't. Some long term health insurance policies pay for day care. Does she have one? If she does I will be glad to fill out any paperwork to help her get it."

"No, she doesn't have that. I think we could afford one or two days. We are trying to get dad's estate settled now."

"Susan, we have a scholarship available, if needed. You will have to fill out some forms for that, but we do have a little help there."

"Thanks, but I think we can swing it. When may we come and visit?"

31

At this point, I check my calendar and schedule an appointment for them to visit. I make sure I have the correct spelling of their names because I will make nametags for them. I also give specific directions to our program.”

"Susan, I look forward to meeting you and Patsy next week. Please write down this number in case you need it. It is our cell number, and you may call me in case something comes up that day and you can't make it. It is….. Susan, before we hang up, may I pray for you?"

"Yes! I need all the prayer I can get."

I will pray as the Spirit leads me and close the conversation. Depending on what the caregiver's response when I ask if the family members goes to church may cause me not to pray but to say instead that I will be thinking about them or even praying for them. If I get an affirmative response, then I may ask if I can pray right then. You will be amazed at the appreciation a person will give you if you pray. You are inviting Jesus into this crisis situation and giving that caregiver His love and grace. It is powerful!

I hope that by reading through this conversation, you got some ideas of how you will answer the calls you will receive. I don't believe there is any right or wrong way to carry on these conversations, but they do need to be professional, non-judgmental and supportive. You must be true to your program and true to the church's integrity every time you talk with someone. You are representing Jesus to a hurting person and can give a cup of cold water in the way you respond!

Notes:

Chapter 7

Getting the Word Out

Marketing Your Program

Once all off your planning is done, the volunteers are recruited, and you are ready to begin, the questions come to mind, "How do I market this program? What are some strategies I can use to let people know that this program will be opening on such and such a date and will be open, let's say, from 10am to 3pm on Tuesdays and Fridays?"

The first place may seem obvious and is right in front of you: share this with your church! It continues to amaze me how often a church member will tell me that they really aren't sure what Grace Arbor is and what it is that we do there! When we planned our opening, I spent several Sundays sharing. I spoke at all three worship services. I visited adult Sunday school classes with my brochures to hand out. I mentioned that someone possibly had a neighbor, a family member, or a friend who had a need for this program.

I visited our circle meetings and let the leaders know the same information. I went to a couple of social events with the church to spread the word. I spoke to other weekday ministries within the church in case any of the parents at our preschool or PMO had a need for respite care. Once I had exhausted the church, I went outward.

I sent a letter and brochure to all of the area churches. In the letter, which our senior pastor wrote, was information about the program and about me the director. During the following months, I began to contact church leaders, reminding them of our program. I tried to go to speak at some senior events at other churches, but I was unsuccessful at the time because I was busy. This would be a great way to get the word out if you have the time.

I wrote an article for our Methodist newspaper and submitted it with a picture of our new group. This was sent to a wide circulation area. I included my contact information in the article.

I invited a reporter from our local paper to do an article about us. Our program was written up in the Georgia Alzheimer's Association quarterly newsletter.

I visited doctors, senior centers, and any other facility that I felt might deal with older adults with memory impairment. I sent out bundles of brochures to these places so that they were ready to hand out to family members. Keeping these places stocked in the future ensures that they will continue to remember you and will share about you.

Networking with others in senior care is vital. We have an organization in Georgia (I think it is nationwide.) called A Place for Mom. I contacted our local representative to share with her about our program. Assisted living facilities are great contacts because they might refer you. In the future, you may refer them to a family in need.

Believe me when I say: TAKE TIME TO MARKET!! This is time well invested and will pay off as the word spreads about your vital ministry!

NEWS FLASH: FUMCLV LAUNCHING OLDER ADULT DAY PROGRAM!!

Did you know that Alzheimer's disease affects nearly 4 million people in the United States and this number is expected to triple by the middle of this century if a cure or other treatment isn't discovered? Did you know that 161,000 people in Georgia and 57,000 people in the metro Atlanta area are affected by Alzheimer's disease? Did you know that research indicates that most families prefer to keep their loved ones at home yet the caregiver literally puts his or her life on hold to be a caregiver? This is due to the fact that an Alzheimer's victim must be watched 24/7 and can live 3-20 years after diagnosis. Care giving can go on for years.

Second Annual Snowflake Ball

"Baby it's cold outside..."

If you are feeling the blahs of winter and want to dust off your dancing shoes, come to the **Snowflake Ball** sponsored by Grace Arbor on Friday February 20. The Roswell Dixie Kings Band will be playing for us from 1:00-3:00PM down in G36. There will be refreshments and lots of dancing and fellowship. Please join us as we dance away the cold of winter together!

Season's Change Workshop
June 10, 2008
1:30PM
in the Parlor
This special Caregiver's Support Group meeting will address end of life issues and future options in care-giving with a panel discussion.
Please invite anyone you know who might benefit from this seminar. For more information contact Robin Dill @Ext 126 or rdill@fumclv.org

What do the images of a white dress, candlelight, beautiful music, gathered family and friends evoke? If the month of June was thrown in the mix I bet you might guess a wedding! June is typically the month we think of as a wedding month. Grace Arbor folks agree with that statement! We will spend the week of June 25th talking about weddings, reminiscing with pictures and gowns. If you would like to join us and bring your dress, pictures and memories I am scheduling times for people to come and share. Please contact me at Ext 126 or email me at robin@fumclv.org.
On June 29 at 1:15PM in the wedding chapel down in Grace Arbor (didn't know there was one did you?) a renewal of vows service will take place to honor the commitment and love between Tom and Robin Spoon. This precious couple is not a member of FUMC but we feel like they are family! Tom has been in Grace Arbor almost a year. Robin has been attending the caregiver support group. Robin has also been battling breast cancer and is presently going through a year long chemo/radiation protocol. Wh they deal with on a day to day basis is truly what love and commitment is all about! If you would like to join us for that special afternoon please come!
Robin Dill, Director of Grace Arbor

34

Chapter 8

Safety Issues

Naomi on Christian Motorcycle Club Day

Safety is paramount for your program's credibility and longevity. You must, as a director, have eyes everywhere at all times. I can't stress the importance of safety enough! If you pay attention to the details, it will dramatically reduce incidents that may cause falls, illness, and closure. (Now, really, shouldn't Naomi be wearing a helmet?!)

Some of the ideas I will share deal with everyday issues and what supplies and equipment you will need to have on hand. Other ideas will deal with infrequent events, such as a fire drill. As I said previously, pay attention to the details!

Supplies and Equipment:
1. **AED -** This machine, while costly, can be the greatest "life saver" in a cardiac emergency. It is very self-explanatory to run, but one does need training. This can be done when you take CPR classes.
2. **First Aid Kit -** Check with your local hospital nursing coordinator for tips on how to create a usable kit. This should include: gauze, Band-Aids, and Clorox Wipes.

3. **911 directions for someone to call in case of an emergency -** I have these typed out and on the wall in our program area. It gives simple directions on what to say and where exactly we are located in the church. In the height of an emergency, you may forget details or become confused. These directions are invaluable.
4. **Files on every participant to be kept with you at all times -** These files should contain the family's wishes for which hospital to transport to if 911 is called. This file should also have information about allergies to drugs and foods, a picture of the participant, and any other information that would be vital to the paramedics or you as you care for that person.
5. **Wheel chairs and walkers -** A few extra wheel chairs need to be on hand in case of fire drills or actual fire. They will also be relevant to have on hand if someone becomes weak and can't walk a distance, say to the bathroom.
6. **Extra clothing provided by the family and extra Depends if they wear them** Toileting accidents are going to occur. Extra clothing will help you in preserving the dignity of your participants. Good Will stores are a great source for extra pants to have on hand. Also keep gloves and wipes in the bathroom.

You need a clear policy about participants attending when they are ill and what you will do if someone becomes ill during the day - No one on staff is a medical professional. If a participant shows signs of illness or infectious disease, the director will contact the participant's caregiver, advising her/him to pick up the participant. Please keep participant at home if temperature is above normal.

Sickness and accidents resulting in physical injury or suspected physical injury will be reported to the director who will arrange for appropriate medical attention. The caregiver of the participant will be immediately notified or emergency actions will be taken. If determined to be necessary, transportation to the hospital will be obtained by calling 911. An accident report will be filed with the signature of the caregiver.

7. **Make sure you have extra phone numbers of someone other than just the direct caregiver.** I had a situation in which I called for two hours when a caregiver failed to show up at pick-up time. She had given me an alternate number - her cell - but no family or neighbor's number. We had to go to her house and found her asleep!! It was a very scary scenario for us as well as for the participant. This was a detail I had failed to check when I received paperwork from this family. It was a tough situation for me, but I learned a great lesson!!
8. **Extra sweaters/sweatshirts or shawls -** Without fail, someone will come to your program one day without an extra layer of clothing and will become chilly. For their well-being, having some "coverings" on hand will make them feel good.
9. **Boxes of tissues at all times**

NOTE: Be aware of any participants who may get choked as they eat.

People with Alzheimer's disease sometimes bolt their food. Keep yourself and volunteers aware of who does this and gently remind them to slow down as they eat.

Fire Drills

Fire drills can run smoothly or be one the most hectic things you will accomplish monthly or quarterly. How often you do a fire drill is up to you and the policy at your church or in your state. Here are some helpful hints that will assist you in making it a better experience.

1. Know which participants are able to walk the distance to your "safe spot" and those who can't. For those who cannot, provide a wheelchair or walker. If a wheelchair is required, remember that you will need someone to push that wheelchair. Do not allow another participant to help. Use volunteers or other staff to do this.
2. Have ambulatory participants paired with volunteers - one hand holding a volunteer's hand.
3. Designate one person to always be the "lead" person. This person will open the door and lead the group out to the safe spot.
4. Some programs use a long rope for everyone to hold onto. I consider this to be demeaning and could be a safety issue if the rope becomes slack and causes someone to trip and fall.
5. Have a place for all to sit down at your safe spot - a picnic table or benches.
6. You as the director need a "Fire Drill Document" that records information about the drill. You will find a copy in the **Form Section**. Take this with you and fill it out on the spot. File it as a permanent record.
7. Take all your files about your participants and a cell phone with you in case of an emergency.
8. You, as the director, will be the last one out the door, having checked the bathrooms and any other places that your participants may be at the time of the drill. When you get outside, take roll to be certain that all are present and accounted for in the "safe spot".

Notes:

Chapter 9

Programming Ideas

The guys on "Talk like a Pirate" Day

As I began to plan Grace Arbor, I spent time visiting programs around Atlanta to see what they were doing. I asked questions to help me make wise decisions about content and quality. Each Congregational Respite program had some similarities and a lot of differences. I am discovering that those differences are based on the gifts, talents, and experiences that we as directors bring to the table. For example, one program had on staff a professional storyteller. She used her gifts to weave stories into the day and the day's topics. Another program had a vivacious director who loved to sing and dance. She had a rousing sing-along at the end of each day. My suggestion to you as you plan your days is to look at your gifts and talents. Where you are lacking, look for gifted volunteers to supply aspects of your program where you aren't personally gifted. You do not have to be able to do it all; surrounding yourself with gifted volunteers and support staff will take your program to a new level.

One of the decisions you will need to make up front is the time frame in which your program will be open each day. Remembering that memory-impaired adults can have difficulty "getting going" in the morning as well as "sundowning" in the afternoon will help you to plan

your day accordingly. We decided on a five-hour day from 10am until 3pm. We felt that this fit in with our caregivers' schedules and the traffic demands around Atlanta.

As you plan the time, you need to decide what components you want to bring to your day. Because one of my spiritual gifts is teaching, I plan a written devotional almost daily. I do this in a format in which everyone can participate in reading and sharing in topic-related questions.

Your space area will dictate some of your scheduling times. We are fortunate to have a fenced toddler playground that is on level ground. We have utilized "space sharing" by creating some raised flower beds and other planting areas for different projects. Right now as I write, a bed of sweet potato vines is growing, and a newly sewn bed of gourds is (hopefully) sprouting. These plantings are part of our programming. I believe in purposeful programming: each thing we do has a cause and effect with the desired result being a joy-filled, meaningful experience.

The sweet potato bed was an outgrowth of a discussion booklet done in March. As a group, we learned how to root sweet potatoes, and we learned about their nutritional benefits. We reminisced about gardening and cooking. After reading the discussion booklet, each participant was given a sweet potato, tooth picks, and a clear cup of water to begin the rooting process. We wrote names on the cups so that everyone could keep track of their potato's progress. In a few weeks after the potatoes sprouted vines, the vines were then placed in water and allowed to grow roots. When the vines were fully rooted, we planted them outside in a prepared bed. We are presently watching them grow. We did an experiment to see whether, if we planted a piece of potato, it would root and grow a vine. In 120 days we will harvest the potatoes and cook with them. Last year we made sweet potato biscuits for our Pastor Appreciation luncheon. This is a small example of the meaningful activities you can plan to do. I will share more under the "Activity" section.

We have evolved into the following schedule in a 5 hour day:

8:30am   **Director Set up/Volunteer Arrival**

This time is used for setup. We put cloths on tables and put out placemats, name cards with holders, silverware, and napkins. We decorate the room to make it look like home: quilts on the walls and extra seasonal décor to make the room inviting and fun. We sometimes put up a puzzle table. After we get everything set up, we take 15-20 minutes to share prayer concerns and pray for our day. The most important thing we do is to ask the Holy Spirit to come and empower us and to be present with us during the day.

10-10:30am   **Arrival and Snack**

Participants arrive, and we gather at the table for conversation and a snack.

10:30-10:40am   **Transition Time for Devotionals**

Participants and volunteers move from table to chair circle for devotions. Participants are recruited to help pass out hymnals and to bring in chair cushions. Volunteers clean up the table.

10:40-11:15am   **Devotionals**

We begin this time with either prayer or singing. If we begin with singing, I will pray before we do the actual devotion. Devotions can take many forms. (See section on activities.)

After the devotion is over, we might sing another hymn or two and close with prayer. A good transition to the next section is a time for everyone to hug.

11:15-11:55am   Movement

Movement can be a combination of exercises and games that stimulate the body and mind. See activity section for ideas.

11:55am-12:05pm   Bathroom Break and Hand Washing

12:05-1pm   Lunch

Plan on this being a relaxing time - not rushed. This may be your participants' best meal of the day.

1:00-3:00pm   Afternoon Activities

Activities are combined with movement and bathroom breaks, as needed. One bathroom break may fall right after lunch before afternoon activities commence. Afternoon activities offer a lot of creative options. See activity section for ideas.

Notes:

Chapter 10

Activities

Mixing Sweet Potato Biscuits

Quality activity programming takes time. Creativity takes time! The dividends of time invested in planning will pay off as your program expands and grows as a result of your planning. How you plan brings about the uniqueness, desirability, and marketability of your program.

Programming that is meaningful and purposeful should meet the needs and abilities of your participants. Activities should foster enjoyment, engagement, success, and a feeling of accomplishment. Thirty to forty-five minute transitions should be planned for people with dementia to help decrease the opportunity of behavior challenges.

Activities can be changed due to the functioning level of your participants. Higher-functioning participants can handle higher-level activities while those same activities, when presented to lower functioning participants, would result in confusion and possible behavior challenges. Activities can target a group or an individual. All should result in success for the participant.

When an activity fails, look at it as a learning opportunity. Ask yourself, "Why did it fail? What could I have done differently? Were my participants having a bad day? Did I fail in my

explanation of the activity?" All these questions will provide valuable planning insight for future activities.

Activities as a Whole

Activities are the "meat and potatoes" of your day. They are what provide the stimulation and enjoyment that cause your participants to want to return to your program. They are what you "do" while you are together. From the minute your participants arrive until the time they go home, they are doing activities. Some require intensive planning, like a Veterans Day event. Others are a natural part of the flow of the day, like morning snack. Each activity must be thoughtfully planned out as to how it will fit into your day's schedule.

Some activities will be done as part of your daily routine. Snack and lunch will occur daily. Others will be done less regularly, like a service project or a particular game like "Jeopardy". You will find activities that certain groups love and want to do over and over. You may give a different "mix" of people those same beloved activities that some had loved and will find that these same activities do not work with your present mix of people. Those activities can be a potential flop. You will not throw those out, though, because you will have a new mix of people to whom you can reintroduce an activity and find that it is a "hit".

My philosophy on activities is to try something at least once, maybe twice. The crazier and "out of the box" type the better. Why? It will potentially be the most stimulating and bring about the most reminiscing of other times in your participants' lives. For example I do a yearly "apple pie making" day. It is messy, tiring, a little costly, and time-consuming on the set up. I have done it with a small group of 5 people, as an intergenerational activity with preschoolers, and with a large group of 15 participants. Each group has been successful because it is different, physically and emotionally stimulating, and I make it fun. I tell them stories of how my parents had an apple pie day. Then I tell them how my daughter and I spent apple pie days with my dad when mom had dementia. I then I ask them about their experiences with baking. This apple pie day has become a tradition and has even turned into a service project because we serve these pies at the Pastor Appreciation Luncheon we do in October to honor the pastors of our church.

On the same note, I tried a winter craft that was a total flop and will never be done again! It was a huge learning experience, however, so it was well worth the flop. It taught me to completely communicate with my volunteers what I need for them to do. It taught me to do a craft in small steps with minimal "stuff" on the table so my participants won't get confused. It taught me to think like one who is memory-impaired as I plan the project to see how far I need to go in my preparation. It reminded me that I really don't like to do crafts!!! But I don't have to if I have a staff member or volunteer who does!!

This activity section will be a culmination of ideas I have gotten from magazines, other publications, brainstorming with staff and volunteers, and from other directors of programs. I am thankful that the Holy Spirit gives me creativity to "run" with an idea and turn it into an activity. My prayer for you is that you will yield yourself to His guidance and allow your creative juices to flow!! Don't be afraid to try something. Just do your planning on the front end.

When the activity is over, then evaluate it. If it was successful, ask yourself why. If it flopped, ask yourself how you could have done it differently, or was it just the mix of people. Through prayer, trial and error, reading, and always seeking, you will develop a fun and interactive program.

Activities can fall under a number of categories and can be as creative as time, resources, and the imagination will allow. Just because an activity fails doesn't mean it was time wasted. Continual assessment helps in making a future activity successful. Asking questions (such as "How could I have done this differently?" "How was my explanation of the activity?" "Was someone having a bad day?") will help to make future activities more meaningful.

Activities can be structured into the day's programming, which is what I do at Grace Arbor. I have my time slots available as to what might happen during the day and look for activities that will fit that schedule.

Notes:

Chapter 11

Daily Activities

"Healing Hooves" Presentation
Wanda is brushing Casper who is a rescued miniature horse.

I use "Creative Forecasting Magazine" to help me set themes for a certain day or for a particular activity. I chart my month to the days Grace Arbor will be open and then begin to build into the month, based on the day's theme. I break my day into components and then begin my planning based on those components. For my program, I know that I will always schedule a devotional/hymn sing time as well as an exercise time. My exercise time may happen 1 or 2 times during that day, and it will include body as well as mind exercises. There will be bathroom breaks and meal and snack time. If we have a lot of movement scheduled, I will try to schedule some "downtime" in the form of a discussion book, story sharing, reminiscing about a topic, or outside entertainment.

As I begin to plan based on a theme, I look at resources readily available, consider outside resources if needed, and ask for help from those gifted in a particular area. If someone from another program did a meaningful activity that they will share with me, I will try to "change it up" to fit my program's needs. Example: Wedding Day was developed after another successful event took place with a group in the church..

At all times, I am considering my participants' level of engaging in the activities and whether or not it will be meaningful. If an activity is strictly geared toward women, I will not consider it on a day that men will attend. Example: Lip Appreciation Day

As I plan, I also have to consider my budget. I also have to consider what resources I have to purchase or what paid entertainment I have to plan for each month. As I plan, I also need to be aware of people who might be able to donate something or volunteer their time to help with an activity.

My goals for each day are these:
1. To honor and glorify God
2. To provide love, acceptance, and joy to the participants
3. To provide a service opportunity for the volunteers of the church and community to use their gifts and talents at Grace Arbor
4. To provide opportunities for the participants to feel accepted, purposeful, independent, , and successful, - and to laugh!

Example:

National Pickle Day

1. I created a devotional that tied into that theme (believe it or not). I did this in the form of a discussion booklet in which the participants can read and share answers to questions related to the devotion.

2. As a group we made Reuben sandwiches (Sauerkraut is a pickled cabbage.) I purchased rye bread, sauerkraut, Swiss cheese, Thousand Island dressing, and pastrami. I used an electric skillet to grill the sandwiches. We made the sandwiches in an "assembly line" with someone getting 2 pieces of bread, another putting the dressing on the bread, another adding cheese, someone else putting on the pastrami, another adding the sauerkraut, and the last person putting on the top slice with margarine. My highest-functioning person helped me "grill" and the lowest helped a volunteer set the table. The whole time we are doing this we are sharing about times we have made lunch for others, what our favorite kind of sandwich is, etc. This was a movement activity because most stood and worked on the assembly line.

3. I created a discussion book about pickles by going on the National Pickle website and downloading information. We had a circle discussion about pickles, and it led up to our pickle-making activity. It gave us an opportunity to have "down" time and to enjoy sharing about pickles and laughing at the crazy things you could make with them!

4. We made pickles by slicing cucumbers, making our "sauce", mixing them together, and putting them in storage containers. There was a safety factor to consider when I planned this activity. We were using serrated knives to slice the cucumbers. I considered who was able to use one before we began. If someone couldn't use a knife, then they were given other jobs to do, such as washing the cucumbers, mixing the spices and the vinegar together, and spooning the "pickles" into the containers.

This was a highly successful day and one I wrote an article about that went into the church newsletter. After all, when one's last name is *DILL,* it is imperative that we salute National Pickle day!

Chapter 12

Spiritual Activities

Renewal of Vows Service Fran and David Schandel

As I mentioned previously, one of my spiritual gifts is teaching. I have been a Sunday school teacher, a neighborhood Bible study leader, and a lover of God's Word for many years. Spiritual activities stimulate me because they provide an avenue to share my love of Jesus Christ and His Word in creative ways. I use many resources during my devotional times; I try to change things around so we don't get into a rut, and so that it stays fresh and stimulating for my volunteers. We do spiritual activities daily for several reasons:

1. Most of our participants are no longer attending weekly worship services.
2. Spiritual activities bring out the truths that were sown into hearts and minds a long time ago. Most of our participants grew up going to church. They were accustomed to singing and reading Bible stories when they were younger.
3. Opportunities for sharing and healing happen during our devotional times. I will never forget the time that we were doing a devotion on a topic that had to do with loss. One of our participants shared about his young son's death and how it led to his becoming an alcoholic and how Jesus set him free. It was a powerful testimony that came about because of God's Word being opened and shared.

4. Daily devotions bring unity and love into our circle. We have many denominations represented in our groups. We learn about our differences and similarities, and we always end our time with some demonstration of love - a hug or a hand shake. It truly sets the tone for the rest of the day.

Our spiritual activities take approximately 45 minutes. We begin with prayer, move on to singing 2 to 3 hymns, share the Word in some form, perhaps sing a few more hymns, and end with prayer. I try to give a direct verbal signal to begin and end our devotional time so that they know we have transitioned into and are transitioning out of this time. We stay in the same spot after devotions most days and do our morning exercises. Verbally transitioning helps cue them for another activity. Some days when we end our devotion time with a "hug 3 people," that is the verbal cue. One of my participants brought the importance of this to me, and I try to do this daily.

Spiritual Activity Equipment and Resources

1. **1 ½ inch binder with large print hymns in non glare plastic sleeves** - I copy hymns at 125% for large print. I put stickers on the bottom right hand side with the page number. A table of contents is at the front of the book with page numbers so people can look at the list and pick a favorite hymn.
2. **A calendar with different Jewish and Christian holidays identified through out the year** - Having a calendar with Holy days is a way of incorporating different ideas into your devotionals. I try to do a devotional booklet about each of the Jewish holidays. It is interesting and helps them to understand their heritage.
3. **Various Chicken Soup for the Soul books or Stories for the Heart books** - I use these books all the time as an extra part of my devotional time. I will pick a topic for a devotional and then look through my books to see if I can find a story that goes along with my devotional. My participants love to hear stories.
4. **Children's Picture Books** - Every fall and Christmas I pull out several children's books to share with my group for devotions. I use a beautiful book when I share about St Francis of Assisi. I share a Stephen Kellogg book when I talk about the life of John Chapman (Johnny Appleseed). I share at least one children's Christmas book a day during advent because the wording, message, and illustrations are pleasing and easily understood. When I introduce the books, I try not to make the hearers feel as though they are being treated like children, but I let them know that the particular book I am about to share says it best!
5. **The Message Bible along with your favorite translation of the Bible** - When I create devotional booklets, I use the **Message Bible** most often as the translation for the booklet. It is written in language that is easily understood and is a fresh presentation. If I create a booklet that has a familiar Psalm, like Psalm 23, I will use the King James translation because it is what the participants will remember.
6. **The book Full Circle, *Spiritual Therapy for the Elderly* by Kevin Kirkland and Howard McIlveen** - This is a valuable resource for your program and devotional time. It has great topical ideas, scriptures, hymns, and songs.
7. **A piano, a piano player. and someone to lead the singing** - You may not be a singer, but you can recruit a volunteer to lead the singing part of devotions. Hymns can be sung

a capella or along with CD's, as well.

8. **Props if you are going to "act out" a scripture** - I rewrote the Good Samaritan in a modern-day version, and we act it out. It has become a favorite of ours to do.

Spiritual Activity Ideas

1. **Devotional Booklets -** This is a concept that I learned from Dr. Cameron Camp's program, *Montessori Method for Dementia Patients*. I create booklets that include topical questions along with a scripture that is based on a theme. We begin by discussing the cover artwork and exploring the message behind the picture. I choose my "readers" from among the participants, and, if I need extras, then I use the volunteers. I will have a participant read one page, and, if there is a question, I ask them to pause after the question. If we spend a lot of time on the question, I will redirect the participant who is reading to where we stopped prior to the question. Some ideas I have used for devotions come from a favorite scripture, what is going on in the calendar, or the season of the year we are in. On the first day of fall, I do a devotion on "Change". During Holy Week, we do a devotion "Saying Goodbye". Visual props brought in during this time are very effective.

2. **Scripture turned into a play or interactive reading -** As mentioned previously, I rewrote the story of the Good Samaritan in modern language, and we act it out. Interactive reading can be done with everyone reading a Psalm aloud together.

3. **Communion -** Twice a month we have a Communion service. I utilize retired ministers, as well as the ministers on staff at our church, to conduct the liturgy. The format is printed in large print (20-22 Arial Font).

4. **Brainstorming and Writing Prayers and Psalms -** We love to brainstorm as a group. This is an effective mind activity that can turn into a spiritual activity. Our group has written a Psalm of praise in response to a devotion; we have written prayers that have been used as gifts; we have taken words and brainstormed acrostic poems. (See Harvest Blessings.) We brainstormed this acrostic and then turned it into a poem for a non profit clinic which is located next door to our church. We framed it and presented it to the clinic as a gift. We also made bookmarks with the poem on them for the staff.

5. **Celebrating Holy Days.** We celebrate several Holy Days in our program. The most time intensive is our Seder meal which we celebrate on Maundy Thursday. This is a whole-day activity with many components. Some of the other days we celebrate are Thanksgiving, Christmas, Easter, Marriage, Rosh Hashanah, Yom Kippur, Purim, and Sukkot.

Notes:

Helping the needy,

Assisting the poor,

Recovery bringing,

Volunteers galore!

Energetic staff,

Sincere in love,

Trustworthy and honest;

Beneficial results from above,

Loving the patients,

Excellent in care,

Superior in giving,

Supporting everywhere,

Intelligent thinking,

Nurturing of man,

Godly in spirit,

Serving with helping hands!

With love, Grace Arbor
October, 2008

Chapter 13

Mind Activities

Creating Memory Books

Mind activities are ones that stimulate our participants mentally, involving cuing, questioning, reminiscing, and encouraging. It will require you to allow time between questions for the thought process to occur in a memory-impaired person. It will require you to help "save face" for your participants by encouraging another to help out with the answer.

Timing is everything when you do mind activities. They can be fun or frustrating. Know your audience and give short introductions to each activity and use short questions. Always give an example.

Mind activities can be a springboard to other activities. Brainstorming a list of seasonal words can be the beginning of a BINGO game. That same list can become a gift in the form of a poem when it is expanded. A word can become a game to see how many words the group can come up with from one word. A grid can be used to stimulate a person's mind to share a memory of an event or feeling.

NOTE: We could include our devotional time as a mind activity, but we won't for the purpose of this chapter.

Mind Activity Ideas

1. Brainstorming

Brainstorming is a group activity. An introduction is given to the group that goes something like this: "Today we are going to brainstorm about Thanksgiving. What comes to mind when you think about Thanksgiving?" As the participants begin to give you words, you write them down on a white board or cling sheet. Remind your volunteers ahead of time that this activity is to stimulate the *participants'* minds. If they get stuck, *then* the volunteers will be called upon. Have a volunteer record the word list; this can be used for several activities, such as categories in Jeopardy, words in Bingo, and words for Hangman or Twister.

2. Grids

Grids are used as an activity to bring about reminiscing. (See Grid at end of the chapter.) A grid can be made on a large white board or on a sheet of paper at a table. The premise behind a grid is that the person is connecting a topic with an action and recalling a memory about the connection.

Once the grid is in front of your group - either in the form of the white board or individual sheets - show how to use it by giving an example: "I will close my eyes and put my finger on a spot on the grid. Where my finger lands will involve 2 words - one from the side and one on the top. Where those words intersect is my topic to share. For example, if I pointed to a place where collecting and accessories intersect, I would be asked to share a story about a time I collected accessories. I might share a shopping experience about looking for shoes to match my wedding dress." Next I will invite a participant to try. If he/she is doing it at the white board, the leader will invite the person up in front of the board and then ask him/her to close his/her eyes and point. After a point is established on the grid, read what it says. If he/she is using a paper grid, have a volunteer see where his/her finger landed. Give him or her the phrase and ask if he/she has a memory relating those 2 words.

Grids can be done around the seasons or monthly topics. They also can involve feelings as well as actions. You can use some of your brainstormed words to be the top part of your grid.

3. Bingo Creating

On your computer, using the "Power Point" program, create a 9-grid. I make at least 10 different grids depending on the length of the word list. I copy on plain paper and laminate them. On a sheet of paper, I create clues that go with each word on the grid. These clues can be transferred to index cards and shuffled before you begin. Select one of your participants who reads well as the person who gives the clues. The rest of the participants must answer the clue and then look to see if the word is on their grid. If it is, it is marked with a button. The winner is the first to fill his or her grid.

4. **Hangman.**

   Hangman is a game we play on a white board. It is very similar to the child's version where a word or phrase is thought of and then dashes representing letters are written under the symbol of the "gallows". The participants are told the category of the word, for example "winter" and how many letters are in the word or phrase. An example of phrase might be "Winter Wonderland". I would then say this is a two word phrase with six letters in the first word and ten letters in the second word. I will go around the circle and ask for letters from the participants. If they guess a letter or letters correctly, I write it on the dash where it belongs. Give the person the opportunity to solve the word or phrase. If the letter is guessed incorrectly, then begin to draw your person hanging from the gallows. Make sure you write the letter to the side so you and your participants can keep track of letters given. The word or phrase is solved when someone guesses it correctly. You will be amazed at how much your folks will enjoy this simple activity. If a person who is lower functioning is in your group and has a hard time coming up with a letter, ask them to give you the first letter of their name. This mind activity is a "filler" if you find yourself with extra time. Or it can be made into a formal activity that is planned. I try to do the topics to go along with the season or month we are in.

5. **Gifts from Brainstorming**

   Words can be powerful. They have the ability to lift our spirits or hurt our feelings. I have found that brainstorming words can be a wonderful gift for caregivers, pastors, and anyone associated with our ministry. These words can be centered around a theme and used as a poem for Thanksgiving, a card that can be illustrated at Christmas, or specialized about a particular person.

   One of the most precious gifts I have received was from the Grace Arbor participants. They brainstormed my name and came up with words that described me, using the letters in my name. One of my volunteers took that brainstormed name and cross stitched it into a beautiful wall hanging!

Notes:

	Ocean	Sand	Shells	Sea Birds	Seafood	Games
Collecting						
Seeing						
Hearing						
Smelling						
Tasting						
Feeling						

Chapter 14

Exercise Activities

"Dancing" at Grace Arbor

Exercise is extremely important to seniors. Our program offers our participants exercise opportunities that most don't get at home. Exercises that strengthen arms and legs will benefit your participants and help them to feel better. I think of exercise as anything that causes the participants to move; it can be in done in a formal exercise activity, during a sing along with feet tapping, dancing, or walking to and from the bathroom or within our program room.

Exercise time should be fun. This is a time to stimulate the body, mind, and spirit. I try to incorporate laughter at any appropriate time. I might explain an activity and then say we are going to do 1000 repetitions. That comment will always get laughter going! The mind is engaged when I ask them to count as we do repetitions. It has been proven that we forget to breathe sometimes when doing exercises, so counting out loud forces us to breathe. If you see someone not counting, give a gentle reminder-*"Don, please count!"*

Exercise can be done with or without music playing. Playing music can present a challenge to people who are hearing-impaired. They may not hear your cues if the music is too loud. On the flip side, the music can stimulate them to pick up their feet if they are marching in a circle to a "march" or to tap their feet to a lively tune if they are sitting.

The following list contains some ideas that have worked for our program in the formal arena for exercise. Having a physical therapist help you to get started is invaluable to the safety of your exercise time. A personal trainer who specializes in seniors would also be a valuable resource for ideas. Research on the Internet will assist you, as well. The National Institute on Aging has a great exercise video. Whatever you do, make it fun, and they will look forward to exercise time!

1. **Arm chair stretching**
   Take your participants through a series of stretches to warm them up. Start with posture and breathing. Then go to hands and arms and then to legs and feet. They are now ready for equipment.

2. **Beanbag exercises**
   Buy 1 pound of dried beans and get a volunteer to sew cloth covers. These are your one-pound weights. They can be used for arm and leg exercises. Even one-pound weights can be effective with seniors to build bone density.

3. **Rubber ball exercises**
   Buy balls at the Dollar store. These are great to use with arm and leg exercises. They also can be used to pass around a circle doing right brain and left brain stimulating activities.

4. **Basketball**
   Buy a child's Little Tyke basketball goal. Shoot baskets either standing or sitting.

5. **Balloon Volleyball**
   You will need a net, balloons blown up with air not helium, and armchairs. Position your chairs so that a partner can be sitting directly across the net from another person. While sitting, bat the balloon back and forth.

6. **Armchair soccer**
   You will need a yoga ball for this. This a great leg exercise. Pass the ball around and across the circle with your feet. You can even play soccer by having 2 spaces around your circle designated as goals. The people on either side of the space are the goalies. Everyone else is trying to score by kicking the ball through the spaces. Watch for high kicks in this game. Remind them to keep the ball on the ground.

7. **Touch Name Three**
   Equipment: Yoga ball with lots of categories written on it in large print
   To play, roll the ball to someone and say, "Wherever your right hand touches, read the word. Now name 3 things in that category." For example, if their hand lands on dogs ask them to name 3 breeds of dogs.

8. **Bean Bag Toss on circle**
   Plastic round tablecloth divided into pie wedges. Write activities all can do like sing Happy Birthday or say The Lord's Prayer. Have one person toss beanbag onto circle into one of the wedges and have another read what it says to do. Everyone does what it says!

9. **Golf**
   Buy a one-hole or multi-hole indoor putting green. Use plastic golf balls and putters.
10. **Parachute with balls**
    Buy a small child's parachute - pop and roll balls in the chute.

Notes:

Chapter 15

Intergenerational Activities

Senior Prom

There is almost a magical atmosphere that occurs when the elderly and the young get together. As an elderly friend once told me when I brought my children for a visit, "I just love young skin!" Intergenerational activities are meaningful and worth the time to coordinate. From babies to youth, look for opportunities to mix ages in your program.

We are blessed to have children at our church on a daily basis, and we have formal and informal activities with these precious children! We invite the children to join us for a story or a game. We ask them to join us for lunch. We do projects and learning activities with them. Many of our children have grandparents who live far away, so we provide them an opportunity to interact with older people who will love them and hug them! The children also bring stimulation and joy to our participants who may not have young grandchildren nearby.

Informally, we see these children as they pass through our room on the way to the playground. This brings visual stimulation; it might prompt a story or a thought; or it might inspire our participants to smile and sing a song.

Some activities we have done in the Intergenerational Setting:
1. Reading a story
2. Playing a game
3. Eating a meal
4. Sharing a snack
5. Breaking a piñata
6. Making apple pies
7. Learning about famous artists together
8. Recreating famous art work together
9. Learning about the families in the orchestra together
10. Making a musical instrument together
11. Learning something about each other
12. Enjoying Senior Prom with our Youth group
13. Hosting our special needs high school class weekly

The opportunities are endless. Please don't miss out on the joy they bring!!!

Notes:

Chapter 16

Activities for the Men

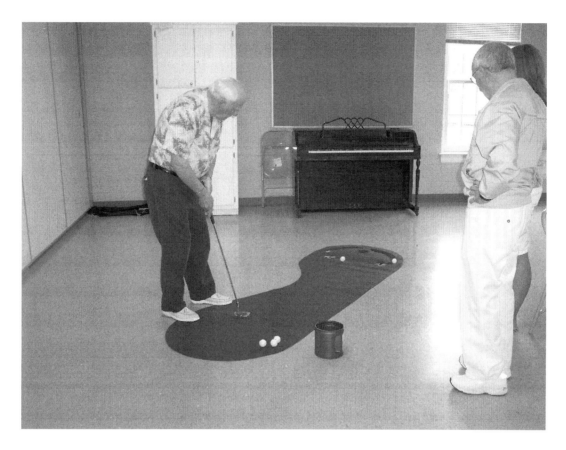

Indoor Golfing

We have a group of men who are very diverse in background and lifestyle. As I plan, I try to come up with some programs that will target their interest as men. It might be sports-related, job-related, or veteran-related. Even though we have both men and women in the program, I still try to plan some things that the men will find interesting. I have discovered that the ladies aren't bored when I do "men activities" if they are well-presented. I did have a bad experience with a Master Gardener who didn't hold their interest because there were no visuals to aid in their experience.

I look for ideas as they share about their past. One thing we do every two years is to celebrate the Olympics. This has become a huge event that stretches over a month's time. We will explore life in the host country by learning about the culture and food. I will try to get someone who has been to that country to come in and share. We have an "Opening Ceremony" with entertainment and a parade of athletes. We will have devotions that go along with the theme of teamwork, winning and losing, and any other theme that relates to a sporting event. We also have venues in which we will actually compete to win medals! We have had a tremendous amount of fun with this activity that typically appeals to our men.

When you do your interview process with your caregivers, ask questions about their loved ones' lives. You will glean a host of ideas from that interview alone. Bringing in someone to whom they can relate will make their day, as well as yours, as you see the joy this experience has brought them!

Other ideas for activities for the men:

1. Bring a famous sport personality and have him or her share about life in sports. Use props as visuals. For example, if the person was a professional football player, you may bring in a football, helmet, and cleats.
2. Do a project, such as woodworking or painting.
3. Celebrate Memorial Day and Labor Day.
4. Include a Veterans Day program.
5. Do a sports activity, such as bowling, golf, shuffleboard, or baseball.
6. Do a service project.
7. Have the men share about their careers. Encourage them to bring in any mementos or pictures.
8. Look at current editions of *Creative Forecasting* magazine. This publication has a monthly section entitled "For the Men".

Notes:

Chapter 17

Activities for the Ladies

For the Ladies

We were fortunate when we added a fourth day to our program. For a year, our fourth day was designated as "Ladies Day". Only ladies attended, and this afforded us a unique opportunity to bless them with activities specifically designed for them.

I will never forget the day that we had two Mary Kay beauty consultants come to do facials with our ladies. We had such fun. One gal looked in the mirror and said, "I never knew I had a mustache!" We laughed ourselves silly!

We have done manicures, facials, antique doll sharing, craft projects, and cooking activities, to name a few. We try to target activities that are meaningful to them in their lives as women. We try to build them up and encourage them in this season of their lives as women. It became more challenging as we began to have the need for a few men to attend on that fourth day. We still do activities for our "Ladies", but it is not quite the same as when it was strictly "us girls".

As I mentioned earlier with the men, you will need to find out about the ladies' pasts when you interview caregivers and try to work that information into your activity planning.

Other ideas for activities for the ladies:

1. Manicures or "satin hands"
2. Facials
3. Vintage clothing sharing
4. Antique dolls
5. Quilting, crocheting, or knitting demonstrations
6. Letter writing to soldiers
7. Intergenerational projects with children
8. Cooking together

Notes:

Chapter 18

Seasonal Activities

"Los Posadas" celebration during Christmas
Piñata Breaking

Seasonal activities are those that occur once a year and extend the normal day into something extra special. The best way to plan for these seasonal activities is to draw on your personal experience as you have celebrated different holidays. A good calendar with special days marked on it is a must-have for doing these types of activities. I have found that "Creative Forecasting" magazine has a wonderful calendar each month that highlights special days that are fun to celebrate.

To plan seasonal activities, decide on a theme that you wish to focus on. You might try to focus all the activities of the day around a theme, tying in your devotional, exercise, afternoon activities, and even the food. For example, I do "Christmas around the World" each Advent season. Each day focuses on a particular country. I look for stories, music, food, and craft activities that relate to that country. There might be an advent hymn or two from that country, as well. It is a fun month to plan. I then extend the invitation to the congregation because someone's heritage might be from one of these countries. One of my participants might have ancestors from a particular country and have a special ornament or story to share. This theme has become rich in the activities we share and gives us a greater appreciation of how people all around the world celebrate Christmas.

Other seasons to celebrate are winter, Valentine's Day, St Patrick's Day, Lent and Easter, Mother's Day, Father's Day, Fourth of July, Memorial Day, Labor Day, start of school, Veterans' Day, and spring, fall and summer. There are so many ideas for activities to do for these seasons. You can spend the month of February doing Valentine or "love"-related activities. We celebrate one week in June as "Wedding Week". We have people share stories, pictures, wedding dresses, and other wedding memorabilia. We end the week with a renewal of vows service for one couple in our program. This has become one of the most meaningful weeks of the year!

Let your imagination, as well as your volunteers' imaginations, explore the "what could we do's" of seasonal activities. Be willing to think outside the box and try something creative. Have fun and explore the Internet for ideas, as well!

Notes:

Chapter 19

Service Projects

Blue Bird Box making for the Hope Clinic

I believe the need to help and to be appreciated never fades. We have all been created for purposeful work, and that need remains as long as we are able to "do". I have found that people with memory-impairment take great joy in helping others as much as anyone else does. I am constantly on the lookout for projects that we at Grace Arbor can help with. Whether it is something as simple as folding cards to something as elaborate as creating birdhouses and painting them, our participants take pride and delight in helping others in need.

As director, your job will be to look for opportunities in which your participants can successfully help others. If you begin a project and the volunteers do it while the participants watch, you have failed. The participants need to be the ones doing the work and interacting. So what if they get their hands dirty or become tired - they have helped and there is deep satisfaction in that!

One of the easiest projects we did when we first started Grace Arbor was doing something to welcome our preschool teachers at the beginning of the school year. I bought apples at the grocery store and gave everyone a towel and apples; the participants polished the apples to give to the teachers. We put a little tag on the apples saying that they were from us. It was easy to do and successful because it was on their ability level.

Another project we are involved in is pillow stuffing. One of our volunteers makes small brightly colored cotton pillows to give to children at one of the local children's hospitals. We help by stuffing the pillows; she then takes them home and finishes them.

Look for ways to involve people in your church with your program in the form of a service project. Ask around to see where needs are and see if you can help. Remember to keep it on the participants' level so it can be a successful project.

Notes:

Chapter 20

Monthly Activities

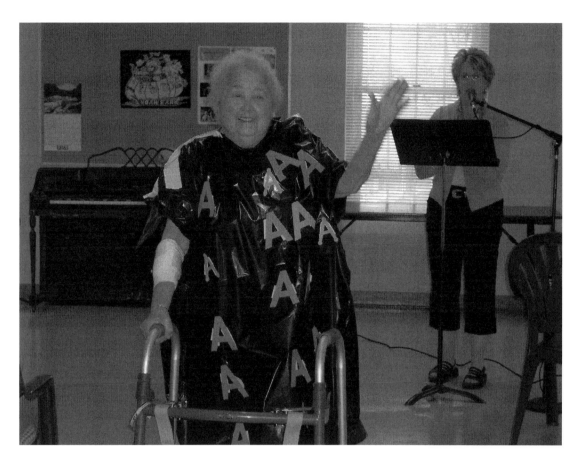

"Bag Dress Fashion Show"
This is one of many that were created by our participants and volunteers. This is an "A" line dress, modeled by Marion Alexander as director Robin Dill introduces her.

As I am writing the chapters on activities, I am suddenly struck with an idea of an activity to do at the beginning of every month. Let the first day of the month be a day in which you brainstorm a list of words having to do with that month. Start with the month itself and then, if a holiday falls in that month, brainstorm words for that holiday. By the end of your brainstorming session, you will have words for many mind and game activities for the month. Save this list in a folder to refer to during the month as you have the need for an activity or a fill in. See the chapters on mind activities and games to expand on this concept.

One of the monthly activities our program participates in is a birthday bag project for a local elementary school. Our Children's Ministry department buys the supplies, and we stuff bags for the faculty and staff of that school. When we are done as a group, we pray over the bags and ask God to bless the recipients!

Notes:

Chapter 21

Musical Activities

Singing with rhythm instruments

Music is a huge part of my program. I have discovered that music touches people with memory impairment deeper than anything else. A song or hymn will bring up a feeling, a memory, or words when a person can't even speak a sentence. Song lyrics will be recalled even when thoughts can no longer can be spoken!

Musical activities can stand alone or be incorporated into other activities such as devotions or exercise. They can be planned out in a discussion book about a famous musician, incorporating a CD of his/her music as a part of the afternoon sing-along.

Musical activities can be intergenerational when songs such as camp songs or typical children's songs are shared. ***"If You're Happy and You Know It"*** and the ***"Hokey Pokey"*** are examples of intergenerational songs. Exploring musical instruments can also be a meaningful intergenerational music activity.

Musical activities can be part of your "outside" programming. Watch your local paper or ask around the church for different musicians who might be able to perform for your program. They can be as simple as a solo instrumentalist, barbershop quartet, swing band, or high school music students. You can plan a "dance" around a swing band's performance. Advertise, invite your congregation, have some simple refreshments and decorations, and you have the makings of a fun time!

Speaking of dances, our program puts on a "Senior Prom" with a theme each summer during Camp Meeting week. We have live music and invite our youth group to join us .We have a blast, and our participants love dancing and interacting with our youth!

Your calendar might declare a certain month as National Piano Month (September). I try to invite certain musicians during these "specific" months to add depth to my programming. This requires planning ahead but is very doable if you are organized!

I have located performers on the Internet and by word of mouth. Other programs in my area try to share ideas, so keep your ears and eyes open. I am always looking for someone or something to entertain our participants.

Notes:

Chapter 22

Outdoor Activities

Planting vegetables in our raised beds

Depending on your program space, you might be privileged to have an area where you can do activities outside. Sitting outside in the fresh air is restorative to many people. Not only does it bring back joyful memories of time with family or friends, but it also is healthy to get some fresh air and sunshine. Fifteen minutes in filtered sunlight gives your body a Vitamin D boost! Outdoor spaces need to be easily accessible to your program, fenced for security, and partially shaded.

One way to get your participants interested in the outdoors is to create a space for them to grow things. We have two armchair-height planters that are eight feet long and two feet wide. We share space with the toddlers in our church so our boxes had to be made from plastic lumber. Although expensive, these planters will not wear out. In these planters, we plant vegetables and herbs in the spring and pansies in the fall. It gives us an opportunity to watch God grow plants and for us to eat and enjoy them as they mature. In another space, we grow sweet potatoes. This project begins indoors and continues outside through the summer months and into the fall. Our harvest day is full of fun and excitement because we never know what we might dig up and what we might see in the garden under the vines. (Yes, last year we saw a snake!!)

Arts and crafts are fun to do outside because of the fresh air. Be mindful of the breeze and papers blowing. Pine cone birdfeeders are a great outdoor fall project because any leftover seed can be scattered for the birds!

We play some games outdoors as well. Plastic horseshoes and bocce ball are fun. Croquet is fun for participants who are not on walkers. Golf is another good activity outside if you have a one-hole indoor green. A chair circle with a parachute is exciting because the sky is the limit to see how high the ball can be "popped up".

Just sitting outside and having a reminiscing activity or afternoon or morning snack can be enjoyable as well. Watching a child's Easter egg hunt or playing will bring joy as well!

Remember a few precautions as you go outside:

1. Drug interactions with sunshine
2. Ground that is not level for walkers and canes
3. Too much wind and cool temperatures
4. Heat and humidity

Notes:

Chapter 23

Games

Summer Olympics Bowling Medal Ceremony

Games are formal activities I do in the afternoon after lunch. They can be done with a small group or with the group as a whole. Some games will require putting participants and volunteers together to form a "team". Other games are played individually. Whenever we play a game, I will declare at the end - whether an individual wins or a team wins - "We are all winners because we played!" I often pass out a chocolate kiss to everyone.

The idea behind games is to engage the whole group, not just one person doing the activity and everyone else "watching". The trick is in getting the spectators to cheer and to encourage if it is an active game like bowling, and to think as a group if it is a game like Jeopardy.

Games should be geared to your participants' level of success. If it is a lower functioning group, take it down a level. The goal is to have fun and to be engaged!

Game Ideas

Bowling
Use a child's plastic (good quality) bowling set with pin and mat.

Golf
A one-hole putting green with plastic balls and several putters (various lengths) can be used.

Touch Name Three
Use a yoga ball with category names written in black Sharpie pen.

Wheel of Fortune	**Jeopardy**
Hangman	**Bingo**
Dominoes	**Speed Stack**
Cards	**Twister**
Balloon Volleyball	**Shuffleboard**

Notes:

Chapter 24

Craft Activities

Painting flower pots to plant pansies

I am going to admit something right up front. I do not enjoy craft projects!!! Thankfully, my assistant director doesn't mind, or we would rarely do them! Crafts are time-consuming but can be very enjoyable and successful if done in small, simple steps. For older adults, you have to pick and choose crafts that aren't too juvenile in their simplicity and will offend their seniority and abilities. If it is too childlike, I refuse to do it. Craft projects need to be explained and demonstrated in small simple steps. Projects need space to be created and space to dry, if painted.

This past week we did a two-step craft project that was very successful. It required 2 steps because it involved painting and planting. We painted clay pots, let them dry during lunch, and then planted pansies in the pots after lunch. The pots were lovely and the caregivers were delighted!

This project was successful for most because it was simple: A clay pot, two paint brushes, and a palette of four colors for each participant were all that was needed. I demonstrated some ideas on a couple of sample pots, and then they started. Some had a hard time picking up their brush and beginning. We encouraged them to dip into the paint and try a design. For most, once they started painting, they did well. A few of them needed some "one on one" help from a

volunteer. We had aprons for all to wear to protect their clothes. The tables were covered with paper to make cleanup easy. Names were written in permanent marker on the bottom of the pots to help identify them.

After lunch, we went back to the same table grouping to plant the pansies. The participants were given a choice of colors and were able to pick the one they wanted to plant. I demonstrated how to un-pot a pansy and loosen the root. Volunteers filled the pot part way with potting soil. The participants could have done this with guidance. They placed their pansy in the pot and added dirt. We did this together step by step together, and it worked great! The end product was a beautiful gift which they had made to give to someone. This craft was on their level - not too juvenile but successful since most of our folks had planted flowers before. It offered reminiscing moments to talk about gardening and planting and learning about roots. The painting allowed for creativity to blossom.

Look for craft magazines in craft stores and utilize publications such as "*Creative Forecasting*".

Notes:

Resource Guide

1. **"Creative Forecasting"**
   P.O. Box 7789
   Colorado Springs, CO 80933
   719-633-3174
   Monthly publication of activities for professionals

2. <u>Full Circle, *Spiritual Therapy for the Elderly*</u> by Kevin Kirkland and Howard McIlveen

3. <u>Montessori-Based Activities for Persons with Dementia (Volumes 1&2)</u> by Cameron J. Camp, Ph.D., Editor

4. <u>Positive Interactions *Program of Activities for People with Alzheimer's Disease*</u> *by* Sylvia Nissenboim and Christine Vroman

5. <u>Alzheimer's Disease *Activity-Focused Care*</u> by Carly R. Hellen

6. <u>Chicken Soup for the Soul</u> books

7. <u>Stories for the Heart and More Stories for the Heart</u> compiled by Alice Gray

8. **Grosfillex Furniture Company**
   230 Old West Penn Avenue
   Robesonia, PA 19551
   610-693-5835   www.grosfillexfurniture.com

9. **Oriental Trading Company**

10. <u>Then Sings My Soul</u> by Robert J. Morgan

11. <u>Exercise: A Video from the National Institute on Aging</u>

12. **Wolverine Sports Catalog 800-521-2832**
    This is a great catalog to order activity equipment. We ordered our bowling, shuffleboard, and other game supplies from this company.

13. The Four Things That Matter Most *A Book About Living*
    by Ira Byock, M.D.

14. End of Life Helping with Comfort and Care National Institute on Aging
    Can be ordered online at www.nia.nih.gov.

Web Sites:

Alzheimer's Association:
www.alz.org

National Council on Aging:
www.ncoa.org/

National Hispanic Council on Aging
www.nhcoa.org

National Alliance on Caregiving:
www.caregiving.org

Free crossword and other puzzle making web site
www.**puzzle-maker**.com

Myers Research Institute - Montessori based Dementia Programming
www.**myersresearch**.org

National Institute on Aging- great exercise video and other resources
www.nia.nih.gov

ARCH National Respite Network
www.archrespite.org

www.fumclv.org
Go to site. Click on Community then Grace Arbor.

e-mail addresses for Robin Dill, Director of Grace Arbor
rdill@fumclv.org and robin.dill@comcast.net